At Issue

| Vaccination

Other Books in the At Issue Series

At Issue

| Vaccination

Lisa Idzikowski, Book Editor

GREENHAVEN
PUBLISHING

Published in 2020 by Greenhaven Publishing, LLC
353 3rd Avenue, Suite 255, New York, NY 10010

Copyright © 2020 by Greenhaven Publishing, LLC

First Edition

Articles in Greenhaven Publishing anthologies are often edited for length to meet page
requirements. In addition, original titles of these works are changed to clearly present
the main thesis and to explicitly indicate the author's opinion. Every effort is made to
ensure that Greenhaven Publishing accurately reflects the original intent of the authors.
Every effort has been made to trace the owners of the copyrighted material.

Cover image: New Africa/Shutterstock.com

Library of Congress Cataloging-in-Publication Data

Names: Idzikowski, Lisa, editor.
Title: Vaccination / Lisa Idzikowski, book editor.
Description: First edition. | New York : Greenhaven Publishing, 2020. | Series: At
issue | Includes bibliographical references and index. | Audience: Grades 9–12.
Identifiers: LCCN 2019022831 | ISBN 9781534506299 (library
binding) | ISBN 9781534506282 (paperback)
Subjects: LCSH: Vaccines—Juvenile literature. | Vaccination—Juvenile
literature. | Vaccination—Social aspects—Juvenile literature.
Classification: LCC RA638 .V27 2020 | DDC 615.3/72—dc23
LC record available at https://lccn.loc.gov/2019022831

Manufactured in the United States of America

Website: http://greenhavenpublishing.com

Contents

Introduction

Most people are familiar with vaccinations and likely, depending on a variety of reasons, have different opinions of the procedure. It's probably safe to say that many children don't like getting "a shot." Most medical professionals and public health officials insist that vaccines protect the receiver from disease. Many parents recognize that getting scheduled vaccinations are a normal part of ensuring the health of their babies. But some parents refuse to vaccinate and insist that vaccinations are risky, pose a threat to well-being, or even cause disease and health problems. And still other individuals proclaim that vaccines and vaccinations go against an individual's personal right to decide about what they do with their own bodies.

Vaccination involves introducing microorganisms into humans in order to develop immunity. The development of vaccines are among history's most important medical breakthroughs. As vaccines became available to the public, horrifying diseases that commonly caused death or debilitating illness were conquered. Of course, not everyone trusted the medical establishment. Toward the late 1700s in the United States, measures were taken to increase faith in the potential to prevent disease. In 1796, British doctor Edward Jenner devised a system of transferring live cowpox virus into a person's arm in order to protect the person from developing smallpox. Doubters lobbied against what seemed like a crazy idea, but prominent individuals saw the benefit. When Jenner's procedure arrived in Virginia, Thomas Jefferson, who was a proponent of scientific thinking and knowledge, championed it. By August 1800, Jefferson had administered the vaccine to more than two hundred of his extended family and neighbors, and over the next few months results were convincing. He determined that the procedure protected against smallpox since none of those so vaccinated contracted the disease.

Knowledge and techniques in medicine continued to improve, and by the twentieth century, the number of vaccines in use had increased, including one for polio, a debilitating and sometimes lethal infectious disease. Up until then, every summer parents dreaded the outbreaks of polio. When Jonas Salk invented the polio vaccine, he became a hero. Then in 1971, the MMR vaccine, for measles, mumps, and rubella, was given. Fast forward to present time, and children can receive as many as twenty-seven shots by the time they reach two years of age.

Not surprisingly, vaccination is a controversial topic. Proponents make a tight case citing numerous statistics about the number of lives saved because of vaccines. According to the World Health Organization (WHO), immunizations currently prevent the death of two million to three million people of all ages each year. Diphtheria, measles, tetanus, and whooping cough are prevented because of vaccines. Many people in the US agree with WHO, as reported by a 2016 survey by Pew Research. A full "73% of US adults said the health benefits of the MMR vaccine are high, while 66% saw the risk of side effects as low. Overall, 88% said the benefits of the MMR vaccine outweigh the risks, while 10% said the risks outweigh the benefits."

Opponents are equally committed and argue against the establishment that promotes vaccination. They often quote parents who say that their children were healthy until they received an immunization. Naturally, parents want to protect their children and act from this standpoint. They want to do the right thing, which can be difficult, especially when very vocal celebrities spread misinformation about vaccines. In 2019, US Surgeon General Dr. Jerome M. Adams publicly went on record to say, "Misinformation about vaccines is still widely reported, so we feel it is crucial to state clearly and unambiguously: Vaccines do not cause autism. That fact was demonstrated again this week in a new study on MMR vaccination by Danish researchers."

Nadine Gartner, a lawyer and founder of Boost Oregon, a nonprofit organization dedicated to the truth about vaccines, says parents are acting out of fear and confusion. Her agency organizes workshops that bring together parents seeking information with a variety of medical professionals. Gartner says that her educators discuss many different topics surrounding the vaccine debate. Their aim is to arm parents with scientific information, calm fears, lessen confusion, and enable parents to make informed decisions. To date, more than three hundred families have attended workshops at Boost Oregon.

Several other factors cause a mistrust of vaccinations. Some people in the United States believe that individuals have the right to make decisions about health independent of how it may impact others and often don't trust scientific experts. A Pew survey showed that 17 percent of Americans believe parents have the right to decide whether to vaccinate their children even if it creates health risks for others. And additionally, not everyone trusts the information provided by medical science. Only 55 percent trust medical experts to give accurate information about the MMR vaccine, leaving the rest to be somewhat trustful or not at all so.

Another big reason that many people don't feel right about vaccinations is actually a testament to the success story of vaccines. Many of the once common childhood illnesses in the US have been done away with exactly because a large proportion of children from several generations have been vaccinated. With hardly anyone getting these diseases anymore, most people have never known any child who suffered or died because they caught measles, chicken pox, or another disease. So, what is the answer—vaccinate or not?

The wide range of discussion topics in this very current debate surrounding vaccines and vaccination is explored in *At Issue: Vaccination*, shedding light on this divisive and ongoing contemporary issue.

1

Pay Attention to Facts, Not Myths, About Vaccines

Dr. Flavia Bustreo

Dr. Flavia Bustreo is a former assistant director-general at the World Health Organization (WHO) for women's, children's, and family health. She has served in a variety of roles at WHO, UNICEF, and the World Bank, and as special adviser to the prime minister of Norway.

Even though the modern-day world is awash with potential information about vaccines and their effectiveness to prevent disease, misunderstandings still persist. Dr. Bustreo points out that even among a group of well-informed audience members at the World Economic Forum, some might say the world's smartest people, many don't understand issues surrounding vaccines. In 2017, 85 percent of the world's children had been vaccinated against measles, which seems to be a large amount. In reality, this is below the idealized target. Bustreo points out the facts about vaccination that could push reluctant parents to immunize their children.

Hans Rosling was a brilliant statistician, medical doctor and communicator, who truly understood the value of immunization.

One of the greatest myth-busters working in public health, he once asked an audience at the World Economic Forum in Davos: "What percentage of children today are vaccinated against measles:

"Embrace the Facts About Vaccines, Not the Myths," by Dr. Flavia Bustreo, World Health Organization, April 26, 2017. Reprinted by permission.

30%, 50% or 85%?" Some of the smartest people in the world mostly got it wrong, with just one in five correctly saying 85%.

Hans told this story to drive home how little most of us understand about the positive impact of immunization. Such a low percentage of correct answers was, he said, clear evidence of preconceived ideas. The folks at Davos weren't just ignorant of the facts—most of them didn't recognize immunization as an incredibly high-impact intervention.

Sadly, Hans, who passed away in February, is no longer around to set the record straight. Immunization is actually one of the most incredible scientific innovations, and has contributed hugely to preventing deaths—mostly of children—and to dramatic rises in life expectancy and economic development. Every $1 invested in immunization returns an estimated $16 in health-care savings and increased economic productivity.

Getting back to the numbers, 85% worldwide coverage for measles is much better than 30% or 50%, but it is still well below the 95% required to ensure population-wide protection. Just a few weeks ago, the Health Minister of Romania reported that 17 children had died in a measles outbreak that has infected thousands of people, most of whom live in areas where immunization coverage is low.

This can happen all too easily when kids don't receive life-saving vaccines, and it is why we need to push much harder to increase immunization coverage (which has increased by only 1% globally since 2010) for all vaccine-preventable diseases, not just for measles.

Stick to the Facts

Despite all the fantastic advances in immunization over recent decades, 1.5 million children still die annually from vaccine-preventable diseases. And not all of our advances are secure. Last year 25 countries reported a net decrease in immunization coverage since 2010.

There are a number of reasons for this. In some countries, consistent supply and cold storage are persisting challenges. In other cases, vaccines are available but myths around them discourage parents from immunizing their children. We need to bust myths and promote the benefits of immunization more widely.

Here Are Five Key Facts About Immunization

Fact 1: Immunization Through Vaccination Is the Safest Way to Protect Against Disease

Whatever you might read or hear, vaccines produce an immune response similar to that produced by the natural infection, but without the serious risks of death or disability connected with natural infection.

Fact 2: It Is Always Best to Get Vaccinated, Even When You Think the Risk of Infection Is Low

Deadly diseases that seem to have been all but eradicated have a nasty habit of making a come-back when immunization rates drop—as we see with the recent measles outbreaks across Europe. Only by making sure everyone gets their jabs can we keep the lid permanently on vaccine-preventable diseases. We should not rely on people around us to stop the spread of disease—we all have a responsibility to do what we can.

Fact 3: Combined Vaccines Are Safe and Beneficial

Giving several vaccines at the same time has no negative effect on a child's immune system. It reduces discomfort for the child, and saves time and money. Children are exposed to more antigens from a common cold than they are from vaccines.

Fact 4: There Is No Link Between Vaccines and Autism

There is no scientific evidence to link the MMR vaccine with autism or autistic disorders. This unfortunate rumour started with a single 1998 study that was quickly found to be seriously flawed, and was retracted by the journal that published it.

Fact 5: If We Stop Vaccination, Deadly Diseases Will Return
Even with better hygiene, sanitation and access to safe water, infections still spread. When people are not vaccinated, infectious diseases that have become uncommon can quickly come back to haunt us.

When people have questions about vaccines they should ask their health providers and check accurate websites for information. Vaccine Safety Net, a global network of vaccine safety websites certified by WHO, provides easy access to accurate and trustworthy information on vaccines. The network has 47 member websites in 12 languages, and reaches more than 173 million people every month with credible information on vaccine safety, helping to counter harmful misinformation.

We are incredibly fortunate to live in an age that has recognized and successfully harnessed the power of vaccines. As Hans Rosling might have said, let's stick to the facts and ensure everyone gets immunized.

2

Debates About Vaccination Are Reduced to Echo Chambers

Chloe Reichel

Chloe Reichel is a writer for Journalist's Resource. She has worked at the Vineyard Gazette, *and her work has appeared in* Cambridge Day, *the* Cape Cod Times, *and* Harvard Magazine.

The public obtains information about vaccines from media and news outlets as much as they do from their personal medical professionals. But it is the debates generated by such stories that is the focus of the following viewpoint. Researchers found that, despite the content, comments attached to the articles revealed deeply polarized views about the general topic of vaccination. Such attitudes inhibit the opportunity for nuanced discussions and information sharing and amplify antagonism.

Comment sections on news articles about the flu vaccine turned into polarized "echo chambers," where like-minded people reinforced and amplified each other's beliefs about vaccination in general, according to an analysis of 2,042 reader responses to Canadian Broadcasting Corporation (CBC) online news reports.

The paper, published in *Vaccine* in March 2019, focuses on themes (discussion of vaccines in general) and rhetorical

"News Stories About the Flu Shot Spawn Debates About Vaccines in General," by Chloe Reichel, Journalist's Resource, March 25, 2019. https://journalistsresource.org/studies/society/public-health/vaccine-debates-anti-vax-flu/. Licensed under CC BY 4.0 International.

devices (such as sarcasm or personal anecdotes) apparent in these comments.

Included for analysis were comments on all text-based news reports that mentioned the flu vaccine published on the CBC's website between September 2015 and October 2016. The comments posted on these articles were extracted and reviewed by three researchers to identify patterns.

The articles generally discussed immunization as a product and/or a service. They tended to share information about flu immunization recommendations and where people could go to get the shot. Articles studied tended not to contain information about risks associated with the vaccine.

The researchers chose to study the flu vaccine in particular for a few reasons. "The influenza vaccine is unique for a number of reasons," said Richard Violette, research coordinator of special projects at the Ontario Pharmacy Evidence Network and an author on the paper, in a phone call with *Journalist's Resource*. "The main component of that difference is its variable effectiveness."

From season to season, the flu vaccine differs in how well it works. According to data from the Centers for Disease Control and Prevention, the flu vaccine for the 2017-2018 season was 38 percent effective; for the 2018-2019 season, preliminary estimates put the effectiveness of the vaccine at 47 percent. "I think that creates this nebulousness around that specific vaccine," Violette said. "It lends to a more difficult decision for individuals."

Violette added that there's complacency around influenza as a disease, too—a sense that it's not a particularly serious illness.

For these reasons, the researchers thought comments about the flu vaccine in particular might offer a window into the minds of those who fall in the middle of the "vaccine hesitancy continuum"— not staunch anti-vaxxers, but not avid vaccine promoters, either.

However, the researchers found that despite the specific focus of the articles, the comments became a highly polarized space, and one that extended beyond the scope of the flu vaccine. Rather, it turned into a place to debate whether to vaccinate at all.

"Comment threads under the included articles largely deviated from article content, instead serving as a forum to exchange information about vaccines and immunization more broadly," the authors write.

"We were a bit surprised by that," Violette said. "We did think initially the comments would be revolving around influenza vaccines specifically."

But online comment sections sometimes evolve or devolve beyond the topic of the article.

As Violette put it, "The forum that opens up beneath rapidly transforms into a place where people can speak about vaccination more generally."

"These online spaces tend to attract the extremely polarized," he added. "Those are the individuals that are the most vocal."

The vaccine hesitant individuals the researchers were first interested in understanding "don't seem to participate in these online spaces," Violette said.

In fact, the participants in the dialogue themselves spurred on further polarization: "The binary is so pervasive in threaded comments that some users actively reminded other users to explicitly position themselves on either side of the debate," the authors write. They cite a comment to illustrate their point: "'Remember, you are either FOR all vaccines OR you are AGAINST all vaccines!'" one user wrote.

Rhetorical Devices

The following bullet points highlight the most commonly used rhetorical devices in the comments and examples of each:

- Sarcasm: "We're talking about flu shots, not polio vaccinations. But sure, just go ahead and take whatever is on offer, no need to apply any critical thinking to make informed choices on your own healthcare. It's not like anybody is in the pharmaceutical industry to make money on you, right?"
- Correcting misinformation: "That is simply not true. Please stop spreading misinformation. Washing hands is great, but

it is certainly not a cure all for influenza. The best defense against spread of the flu is immunization. No other measure even comes close."

- Anecdote: "I've had full-blown influenza once and I never want to feel like that again. It's not at all the same as a bad cold; it's systemic and just plain nasty. That was 20 years ago and I've had my annual flu shot ever since."
- Ridicule: "Cue the big pharma hipsters and soccer mommies who think they know more than doctors and scientists."
- Use of evidence: "Not only is the flu vaccine not a magical 100% barrier to transmitting the flu to vulnerable patients, there is evidence that receiving the recent ineffective vaccines makes individuals more vulnerable to mutated strains of the flu."
- Request for proof: "Source? Evidence? Any proof of this?"
- Analogy: "If you had a 50% chance of winning the lottery, would you refuse to buy a ticket because of the equal possibility you won't win?"
- Knowledge deficit: "More 'aluminum' in a pickle than a dose of flu vaccine. Do you know 'aluminum' (sulfate) is used in water purification systems? So much scaremongering with the word 'mercury' and 'aluminum' due to the level of ignorance about basic chemistry that sadly seems to go hand in glove with the antivaxx mindset."

Though both sides used a number of these techniques, there were key differences in exactly how they used them.

Take, for example, the use of evidence.

Violette called vaccine refusers "experts" at creating and subsequently linking to websites and social media that disseminate their views.

And it's not just the medium, it's also the message.

"The anti-vaxxers have just developed a really great way to communicate in these spaces," he told *Journalist's Resource.*

With regard to trying to dispute these views with scientific evidence, "one of the problems with that is, a lot of the science supportive of vaccination is not really easily accessible to the layperson, whether by content or by access," he said.

For Violette, the most concerning aspect of this polarized debate is the impact it might have on the vaccine hesitant population he and his coauthors initially wanted to study. "We can safely assume there's a large number of individuals who'd qualify as vaccine hesitant … who are passively consuming those dialogues online," he said.

"Effectively, these online spaces, because they are so polarized, it erases any space for people who have doubts, it erases any space for people who have questions," he added. Further, this debate is now "feeding into the assembly of their evidence base on which they could be making their future vaccine decisions."

As Facebook and Instagram move to moderate anti-vaccination content on their platforms, Violette suggested a focus on correct information, rather than moderation, might be the best path forward.

"There is a responsibility to be diffusing the correct information," he said. "Does that mean erasing the misinformation? I'm not sure. Enabling individuals who may not have had the training or education to read scientific literature, to sift through information and be more critical—that might potentially be the role public health needs to play."

And although this study focused on a Canadian news organization, Violette said he believes the findings are generalizable. "At the end of the day the phenomenon of back-and-forth, really polarized comments … I think it's pretty generalizable across the board," he said.

3

Vaccines Protect Against Other Diseases, Too

Christine Stabell Benn

Dr. Christine Stabell Benn is a professor of global health at the University of Southern Denmark. Dr. Benn's research investigates the effects of health interventions and their prospects for overall health. Her focus is on vaccines and vitamins on the population of Guinea-Bissau, West Africa, one of the poorest nations in the world.

The research team headed by Dr. Christine Stabell Benn has come upon a startling discovery: vaccines not only protect against the target disease but they also protect against other, non-intended diseases as well. Research that focused in Africa points to a reduced death rate from the measles vaccination by more than 70 percent, an amount that shows this vaccine works against other death-causing diseases as well. Interestingly, Benn's studies showed that unexpected negative results also occur with certain vaccinations.

A measles vaccine protects against measles infection. By introducing a bit of weakened virus, the immune system learns how to deal with it, so when a real measles virus comes along, it can eliminate it. But does the immune system learn more from the vaccine? Recent research suggests, rather intriguingly, that it does.

Our group first noticed this phenomenon in Guinea-Bissau in West Africa over 30 years ago. We followed a large sample of the population, with regular home visits. The focus was on nutritional status, but as a service to the community, in December 1979, we provided a measles vaccine for all children. The following year, we observed something amazing: the measles vaccine reduced overall mortality by more than 70%—much more than could be explained by the prevention of measles infection, which only caused around 10-15% of all deaths at that time.

During further research, it became clear that the effect of these vaccines on overall health couldn't be explained by their disease-specific effects. Vaccines also affect the risk of other infections. We coined these effects the "non-specific effects" of vaccine.

Two Types of Vaccines

There are two major types of vaccines, live and non-live. Live vaccines contain the disease organism in a weakened form. They create a mild natural infection in the body, usually so mild that there are no symptoms. These vaccines give good protection against the disease they were designed for from the first dose. (Though these vaccines have the very rare potential to cause real disease, particularly in people with compromised immune systems.)

Non-live vaccines contain the killed disease organism or parts of it. They are not very good at stimulating the immune system and usually have to be given with a helper substance, known as an "adjuvant," and in several shots to give disease protection. The non-live vaccines can never create the real disease, so most doctors prefer them over live vaccines.

We have now investigated four live vaccines and six non-live vaccines, in Guinea-Bissau and other low-income countries, as well as in Denmark. A consistent pattern has emerged. The live vaccines reduce death and disease much more than can be explained by the specific protection. But the non-live vaccines, in spite of protecting against the vaccine disease, are associated with negative effects on health, including death, particularly for girls. Here are two examples.

BCG

BCG vaccine is a live vaccine against tuberculosis. It is recommended at birth in poor countries. But newborns with low birth weight are normally vaccinated later. We tested the effect of BCG vaccine on overall health in this group. We randomly allocated Guinean children who weighed less than 2.5kg to receive BCG at birth or the usual delayed BCG.

In the first month of life, deaths from any cause were reduced by more than a third in children who received the vaccine versus those who didn't. Children don't die from tuberculosis in the first month of life. But BCG reduced their risk of dying from sepsis and pneumonia—a purely non-specific effect of BCG, which had nothing to do with protection against tuberculosis.

In sub-Saharan Africa, BCG is often given with delay. Currently, only around 50% of all children, irrespective of weight, receive BCG at birth. If our results are correct, it would be possible to prevent 200,000 babies dying each year simply by making sure that all children received the BCG vaccine at birth.

DTP

Diphtheria, tetanus and pertussis (DTP) vaccine is a non-live vaccine against three serious and potentially deadly diseases. So it has been assumed that introducing it would reduce overall mortality. But when we tested what had happened when the DTP vaccine was introduced in Guinea-Bissau, we were very surprised. In spite of protecting against the diseases, DTP-vaccinated children had fivefold higher mortality than children who didn't receive the vaccine.

We have repeated this finding many times. Protection against diphtheria, tetanus and pertussis seems to come at a very high price: increased risk of dying from other infections, such as respiratory infections, particularly for females. Translated into absolute numbers, the results indicate that the use of DTP vaccine in sub-Saharan Africa may cost tens of thousands of female lives every year.

These are just two examples among many studies done by our team. Besides BCG, we have found beneficial non-specific effects of the live measles, smallpox and oral polio vaccines. And besides DTP, we have found negative effects in females of the non-live pentavalent vaccine (which combines immunisation against five diseases), as well as the inactivated polio, hepatitis B and H1N1 influenza vaccines, and we also predicted a negative effect of the new malaria vaccine in females.

Not many places have the kind of data needed to conduct these studies, but other research groups are now starting to replicate our findings in other poor regions of Africa and Asia. The same patterns have also been seen in wealthy countries. For instance, a recent US study found that the risk of getting hospitalised for other infections was halved among children who had a live versus a non-live vaccine.

The World Health Organisation recently reviewed the evidence for non-specific effects of the live BCG and measles vaccine and the non-live DTP vaccine and concluded that BCG and measles-containing vaccines could reduce overall mortality by more than expected, while higher all cause mortality may be associated with receipt of DTP.

Effect of Vaccines on the Immune System

The immune system has traditionally been divided into the innate and the adaptive immune system, with the innate seen as the first line of defence, with no memory of previous pathogens. The adaptive has been seen as the place where the memory of disease organisms develops, which can be measured in the antibodies the disease creates. The protective effect of vaccines has largely been ascribed to the ability to induce antibodies.

However, recent research has taught us that the immune system is more complex. The innate immune system also learns when exposed to a disease organism. In a recent experiment, we showed that volunteers who received a BCG vaccine four weeks before a yellow fever vaccine had much less yellow fever virus in the blood, and this was because BCG vaccine trained their innate immune cells to become more vigilant. So we now have evidence that a vaccine can change the immune response to subsequent unrelated infections in humans. This goes a long way to explaining how vaccines can influence other diseases and overall health.

Hard to Find What You're Not Looking For

Vaccines have been used for centuries. So if they have such profound effects on the risk of other diseases, why didn't we discover this a long time ago? The short answer is that you can't discover what you're not looking for.

Everybody has been convinced that vaccines only affected the target infection, so their effect on other infections and overall health was not studied. So while there are many studies that show that vaccines have protective effects, there is no data that shows that vaccines only have protective effects.

It is time to change our perception of vaccines: vaccines are not merely a protective tool against a specific disease, they affect the immune system broadly. In the case of live vaccines, the immune system is strengthened. In contrast, non-live vaccines seem to have a negative effect on the immune system in females.

The latter finding is an obvious cause for concern, particularly since it would be undesirable to stop using, say, the DTP vaccine, as it protects against three severe diseases. Fortunately, there is something to do. It appears that if a live vaccine is given after a non-live vaccine, the negative effect of the non-live vaccine may be mitigated. So there is an urgent need for studies testing different sequences of live and non-live vaccines.

Studies into the overall health effects of vaccines are providing new insights about the immune system and how it may be trained by vaccines. Live vaccines seem to be potent immune trainers, and with this new knowledge we may be able to reduce global child mortality by more than a million deaths a year. With smarter use of vaccines, we may also be able to reduce disease and improve child health in wealthy countries.

4

US Vaccines Are Safe—Here's Why

US Department of Health and Human Services

The US Department of Health and Human Services (HHS) is a governmental body of the United States. The agency's mission is to protect and enhance the health of all Americans. To achieve this goal, the agency promotes advances in medicine, social services, and public health.

The US Department of Health & Human Services oversees the US Food and Drug Administration, which ensures the safety of vaccines in the United States. The aim of both agencies is to protect US citizens against unsafe vaccines. Outlined in the viewpoint article are the procedures used to achieve this goal along with the ways that scientists use data to monitor vaccines after they are approved for general use and if there are suspected adverse side effects from vaccinations.

Currently, the United States has the safest, most effective vaccine supply in its history. The United States' long-standing vaccine safety system ensures that vaccines are as safe as possible. As new information and science become available, this system is, and will continue to be, updated and improved.

The US Food and Drug Administration (FDA) ensures the safety, effectiveness, and availability of vaccines for the United States. Before the FDA licenses (approves) a vaccine, the vaccine is tested extensively by its manufacturer. FDA scientists and medical

"Ensuring the Safety of Vaccines in the United States," US Department of Health and Human Services, July 2011.

professionals carefully evaluate all the available information about the vaccine to determine its safety and effectiveness.

Although most common side effects of a vaccine are identified in studies before the vaccine is licensed, rare adverse events may not be detected in these studies. Therefore, the US vaccine safety system continuously monitors for adverse events (possible side effects) after a vaccine is licensed. When millions of people receive a vaccine, less common side effects that were not identified earlier may show up.

Prelicensure: Vaccine Safety Testing

The US Food and Drug Administration (FDA) must license (approve) a vaccine before it can be used in the United States. FDA regulations for the development of vaccines ensure their safety, purity, potency, and effectiveness. Before a vaccine is approved by the FDA for use by the public, results of studies on safety and effectiveness of the vaccine are evaluated by highly trained FDA scientists and doctors. The FDA also inspects the vaccine manufacturing sites to make sure they comply with current Good Manufacturing Practice (cGMP) regulations.

Vaccine Development

Vaccine development begins in the laboratory before any tests in animals or humans are done. If laboratory tests show that a vaccine has potential, it is usually tested in animals. If a vaccine is safe in animals, and studies suggest that it will be safe in people, clinical trials with volunteers are next.

Clinical Trials

Typically, there are three phases of clinical trials. Vaccines that are being developed for children are first tested in adults. The FDA sets guidelines for the three phases of clinical trials to ensure the safety of the volunteers.

Phase 1 clinical trials focus on safety and include 20–100 healthy volunteers. In Phase 1, scientists begin to learn how the size of the dose may be related to side effects. If possible at this early stage, scientists also try to learn how effective the vaccine may be.

If no serious side effects are found in Phase 1, next is Phase 2, which involves several hundred volunteers. This phase includes studies that may provide additional information on common short-term side effects and how the size of the dose relates to immune response.

In Phase 3 studies, hundreds or thousands of volunteers participate. Vaccinated people are compared with people who have received a placebo or another vaccine so researchers can learn more about the test vaccine's safety and effectiveness and identify common side effects.

Clinical trials are conducted according to plans that the FDA reviews to ensure the highest scientific and ethical standards. The results of the clinical trials are a part of the FDA's evaluation to assess the safety and effectiveness of each vaccine. In addition to evaluating the results of the clinical trials, FDA scientists and medical professionals carefully evaluate a wide range of information including results of studies on the vaccine's physical, chemical, and biological properties, as well as how it is manufactured, to ensure that it can be made consistently safe, pure, and potent.

The trials and all other data must show that the vaccine's benefits outweigh the potential risks for people who will be recommended to receive the vaccine. Only if a vaccine's benefits are found to outweigh its potential risks does the FDA grant a license for the vaccine, allowing it to be used by the public.

Postlicensure: Vaccine Safety Monitoring

After vaccines are licensed, they are monitored closely as people begin using them. The purpose of monitoring is to watch for adverse events (possible side effects). Monitoring a vaccine after it is licensed helps ensure that the benefits continue to outweigh the risks for people who receive the vaccine.

Monitoring is essential for two reasons. First, even large clinical trials may not be big enough to reveal side effects that do not happen very often. For example, some side effects may only happen in 1 in 100,000 or 1 in 500,000 people.

Second, vaccine trials may not include groups who might have different types of side effects or who might have a higher risk of side effects than the volunteers who got the vaccine during clinical trials. Examples of these groups include people with chronic medical conditions, pregnant women, and older adults.

If a link is found between a possible side effect and a vaccine, public health officials take appropriate action by first weighing the benefits of the vaccine against its risks to determine if recommendations for using the vaccine should change.

The Advisory Committee on Immunization Practices (ACIP), a group of medical and public health experts, carefully reviews all safety and effectiveness data on vaccines as a part of its work to make recommendations for the use of vaccines. The ACIP modifies recommendations, if needed, based on safety monitoring.

VAERS

Postlicensure monitoring begins with the Vaccine Adverse Event Reporting System (VAERS), a national system used by scientists at the FDA and the Centers for Disease Control and Prevention (CDC) to collect reports of adverse events (possible side effects) that happen after vaccination. Health care professionals, vaccine manufacturers, vaccine recipients, and parents or family members of people who have received a vaccine are encouraged to submit reports to VAERS if they experience any adverse events after getting any vaccine.

Scientists monitor VAERS reports to identify adverse events that need to be studied further. All serious reports are reviewed by medical professionals on a daily basis. VAERS data provide medical professionals at the CDC and FDA with a signal of a potential adverse event. Experience has shown that VAERS is an excellent tool for detecting potential adverse events. Reports of adverse events that are unexpected, appear to happen more often than expected, or have unusual patterns are followed up with specific studies.

VAERS data alone usually cannot be used to answer the question, "Does a certain vaccine cause a certain side effect?" This is mainly because adverse events reported to VAERS may or may not be caused by vaccines. There are reports in VAERS of common conditions that may occur by chance alone that are found shortly after vaccination. Investigation may find no medical link between vaccination and these conditions.

To know if a vaccine causes a side effect, scientists must know whether the adverse event is occurring after vaccination with a particular vaccine more often than would be expected without vaccination. They also need to consider whether the association between the vaccine and the adverse event is consistent with existing medical knowledge about how vaccines work in the body.

VSD

Scientists use the CDC's Vaccine Safety Datalink (VSD) to do studies that help determine if possible side effects identified using VAERS are actually related to vaccination. VSD is a network of eight managed care organizations across the United States. The combined population of these organizations is more than 9.2 million people.

Scientists can use VSD in two ways. First, scientists can look back in medical records to see if a particular adverse event is more common among people who have received a particular vaccine. Second, instead of looking back, scientists can use Rapid Cycle Analysis (RCA) to continuously look at information coming into VSD to see if the rate of certain health conditions is higher among vaccinated people. This second approach is new, and it allows results to be obtained much more quickly.

Vaccine Manufacturing

Once a vaccine is licensed, the FDA regularly inspects vaccine manufacturing facilities to make sure they are following strict regulations. Vaccines are manufactured in batches called lots, and vaccine manufacturers must test all lots of a vaccine to make sure they are safe, pure, and potent. Vaccine lots cannot be distributed until released by the FDA.

5

Vaccinating a Large Percentage of the Population Prevents Infection

Allen Cheng

Dr. Allen Cheng is a professor in the department of epidemiology and preventive medicine at Monash University in Australia and an epidemiologist and infectious disease specialist at the Alfred Hospital in Melbourne, Australia.

Dr. Cheng argues for vaccination by providing examples of what happens in two different cases: treatment of individuals versus treatment of populations. With individuals a variety of things are taken into account. What are the options available, what does the person prefer, and is the individual possibly susceptible to side effects? With entire populations it's different. Cheng maintains that even though it is not possible to predict which person might get sick or might have value in being vaccinated, such as in the case before antibiotics cured pneumonia with 80 percent of people that otherwise would have died, vaccination for large populations is still valid and appropriate.

A recent article in The Conversation questioned whether we should all get flu vaccinations, given 99 people would have to go through vaccination for one case of flu to be prevented.

"Most People Don't Benefit from Vaccination, but We Still Need It to Prevent Infections," by Allen Cheng, The Conversation, June 8, 2018, https://theconversation.com/most-people-dont-benefit-from-vaccination-but-we-still-need-it-to-prevent-infections-97928. Licensed under CC BY ND 4.0 International.

But this position ignores the purpose of immunisation programs: whole populations of people need to take part for just a small number to benefit. So how do we decide what's worth it and what's not?

Decision-Making in Public Health

When we consider a treatment for a patient, such as antibiotics for an infection, we first consider the evidence on the benefits and potential harms of treatment. Ideally, this is based on clinical trials, where we assume the proportion of people in the trial who respond represents the chance an individual patient will respond to treatment.

This evidence is then weighed up with the individual patient. What are the treatment options? What do they prefer? Are there factors that might make this patient more likely to respond or have side effects? Is there a treatment alternative they would be more likely to take?

In public health, the framework is the same but the "patient" is different—we are delivering an intervention for a whole population or group rather than a single individual.

We first consider the efficacy of the intervention as demonstrated in clinical trials or other types of studies. We then look at which groups in the population might benefit the most (such as the zoster vaccine, given routinely to adults over 70 years as this group has a high rate of shingles), and for whom the harms will be the least (such as the rotavirus vaccine, which is given before the age of six months to reduce the risk of intussusception, a serious bowel complication).

Compared to many other public health programs, immunisation is a targeted intervention and clinical trials tell us they work. But programs still need to target broad groups, defined by age or other broad risk factors, such as chronic medical conditions or pregnancy.

Risks and Benefits of Interventions

When considering vaccination programs, safety is very important, as a vaccine is being given to a generally healthy population to prevent a disease that may be uncommon, even if serious.

For example, the lifetime risk of cervical cancer is one in 166 women, meaning one woman in 166 is diagnosed with this cancer. So even if the human papillomavirus (HPV) vaccine was completely effective at preventing cancer, 165 of 166 women vaccinated would not benefit. Clearly, if we could work out who that one woman was who would get cancer, we could just vaccinate her, but unfortunately we can't.

It's only acceptable to vaccinate large groups if clinically important side effects are low. For the HPV vaccine, anaphylaxis (a serious allergic reaction) has been reported, but occurs at a rate of approximately one in 380,000 doses.

An even more extreme case is meningococcal vaccination. Before vaccination, the incidence of meningococcal serogroup C (a particular type of this bacterium) infection in children aged one to four years old was around 2.5 per 100,000 children, or 7.5 cases for 100,000 children over three years.

Vaccination has almost eliminated infection with this strain (although other serotypes still cause meningococcal disease). But this means 13,332 of 13,333 children didn't benefit from vaccination. Again, this is only acceptable if the rate of important side effects is low. Studies in the US have not found any significant side effects following routine use of meningococcal vaccines.

This is not to say there are no side effects from vaccines, but that the potential side effects of vaccines need to be weighed up against the benefit.

For example, Guillain Barre syndrome is a serious neurological complication of influenza vaccination as well as a number of different infections.

But studies have estimated the risk of this complication as being around one per million vaccination doses, which is much smaller than the risk of Guillain Barre syndrome following influenza infection (roughly one in 60,000 infections). And that's before taking into account the benefit of preventing other complications of influenza.

What Other Factors Need to Be Considered?

We also need to consider access, uptake and how a health intervention will be delivered, whether through general practices, council programs, pharmacies or school-based programs.

Equity issues must also be kept in mind: will this close the gap in Indigenous health or other disadvantaged populations? Will immunisation benefit more than the individual? What is the likely future incidence (the "epidemic curve") of the infection in the absence of vaccination?

A current example is meningococcal W disease, which is a new strain of this bacteria in Australia. Although this currently affects individuals in all age groups, many state governments have implemented vaccination programs in adolescents.

This is because young adults in their late teens and early 20s carry the bacteria more than any other group, so vaccinating them will reduce transmission of this strain more generally.

But it's difficult to get large cohorts of this age group together to deliver the vaccine. It's much easier if the program targets slightly younger children who are still at school (who, of course, will soon enter the higher risk age group).

In rolling out this vaccine program, even factors such as the size of schools (it is easier to vaccinate children at high schools rather than primary schools, as they are larger), the timing of exams, holidays and religious considerations (such as Ramadan) are also taken into account.

For government, cost effectiveness is an important consideration when making decisions on the use of taxpayer dollars. This has been an issue when considering meningococcal B vaccine. As this is a relatively expensive vaccine, the Pharmaceutical Benefits Advisory Committee has found this not to be cost effective.

This is not to say that meningococcal B disease isn't serious, or that the vaccine isn't effective. It's simply that the cost of the vaccine is so high, it's felt there are better uses for the funding that could save lives elsewhere.

While this might seem to be a rather hard-headed decision, this approach frees up funding for other interventions such as expensive cancer treatments, primary care programs or other public health interventions.

Why Is This Important?

When we treat a disease, we expect most people will benefit from the treatment. As an example, without antibiotics, the death rate of pneumonia was more than 80%; with antibiotics, less than 20%.

However, vaccination programs aim to prevent disease in whole populations. So even if it seems as though many people are having to take part to prevent disease in a small proportion, this small proportion may represent hundreds or thousands of cases of disease in the community.

6

A Vaccine, Like Any Medicine, May Have Side Effects

College of Physicians of Philadelphia

The College of Physicians of Philadelphia is a medical society in the United States established in 1787. The college's mission is to enhance the cause of health in the US. The college maintains an educational website—The History of Vaccines—to inform individuals about vaccination.

The College of Physicians of Philadelphia maintains that any vaccination, like medications, may cause side effects. What the college asserts is that most side effects are very mild. Details include the number of babies in the US that receive vaccinations and the fact that many babies suffer other incidents in the first year of life that have nothing to do with vaccinations. The viewpoint compares two different vaccinations—one of a vaccine with very few side effects, and the other a vaccine known for its degree of side effects that can be extreme.

A vaccine is a medical product. Vaccines, though they are designed to protect from disease, can cause side effects, just as any medication can.

Most side effects from vaccination are mild, such as soreness, swelling, or redness at the injection site. Some vaccines are

College of Physicians of Philadelphia. (2018). Vaccine Side Effects and Adverse Events. Retrieved from https://www.historyofvaccines.org/content/articles/vaccine-side-effects-and-adverse-events.

associated with fever, rash, and achiness. Serious side effects are rare, but may include seizure or life-threatening allergic reaction.

A possible side effect resulting from a vaccination is known as an adverse event.

Each year, American babies (1 year old and younger) receive more than 10 million vaccinations. During the first year of life, a significant number of babies suffer serious, life-threatening illnesses and medical events, such as Sudden Infant Death Syndrome (SIDS). Additionally, it is during the first year that congenital conditions may become evident. Therefore, due to chance alone, many babies will experience a medical event in close proximity to a vaccination. This does not mean, though, that the event is in fact related to the immunization. The challenge is to determine when a medical event is directly related to a vaccination.

The Food and Drug and Administration (FDA) and the Centers for Disease Control and Prevention (CDC) have set up systems to monitor and analyze reported adverse events and to determine whether they are likely related to vaccination.

Types of Side Effects

To understand the range of possible vaccination side effects events, it is useful to compare a vaccine with relatively few associated side effects, such as the vaccine for *Haemophilus influenza* type B, with a vaccine known to have many potential side effects, such as the infrequently used smallpox vaccine (given to military personnel and others who might be first responders in the event of a bioterror attack).

Haemophilus influenza type B is a bacterium that can cause serious infections, including meningitis, pneumonia, epiglottitis, and sepsis. The CDC recommends that children receive a series of Hib vaccinations starting when they are two months old.

Smallpox is a serious infection, fatal in 30% to 40% of cases, and caused by the *Variola major* or *Variola minor* virus. No wild smallpox cases have been reported since the 1970s. The World Health Organization has declared it eradicated.

The information below about side effects of Hib and smallpox vaccination is from the Centers for Disease Control and Prevention.

Hib Vaccine Side Effects

- Redness, warmth, or swelling where the shot was given (up to 1 out of 4 children)
- Fever over 101°F (up to 1 out of 20 children)

No serious side effects have been related to the Hib vaccine.

Smallpox (Vaccinia) Vaccine Side Effects
Mild to Moderate Problems:

- Mild rash, lasting 2-4 days.
- Swelling and tenderness of lymph nodes, lasting 2-4 weeks after the blister has healed.
- Fever of over 100°F (about 70% of children, 17% of adults) or over 102°F (about 15%-20% of children, under 2% of adults).
- Secondary blister elsewhere on the body (about 1 per 1,900).

Moderate to Severe Problems:

- Serious eye infection, or loss of vision, due to spread of vaccine virus to the eye.
- Rash on entire body (as many as 1 per 4,000).
- Severe rash on people with eczema (as many as 1 per 26,000).
- Encephalitis (severe brain reaction), which can lead to permanent brain damage (as many as 1 per 83,000).
- Severe infection beginning at the vaccination site (as many as 1 per 667,000, mostly in people with weakened immune systems).
- Death (1-2 per million, mostly in people with weakened immune systems).

For every million people vaccinated for smallpox, between 14 and 52 could have a life-threatening reaction to smallpox vaccine.

How Do I Find Out the Side Effects for Different Vaccines?

When you or a child gets a vaccine, the health care provider gives you a handout known as the Vaccine Information Statement (VIS). The VIS describes common and rare side effects, if any are known, of the vaccine. Your health care provider will probably discuss possible side effects with you. VIS downloads are also available through the CDC's website.

Package inserts produced by the vaccine manufacturer also provide information about adverse events. Additionally, these inserts usually show rates of adverse events in experimental and control groups during pre-market testing of the vaccine.

How Are Adverse Events Monitored?

VAERS

The CDC and FDA established the Vaccine Adverse Event Reporting System in 1990. The goal of VAERS, according to the CDC, is "to detect possible signals of adverse events associated with vaccines." (A signal in this case is evidence of a possible adverse event that emerges in the data collected.) About 30,000 events are reported each year to VAERS. Between 10% and 15% of these reports describe serious medical events that result in hospitalization, life-threatening illness, disability, or death.

VAERS is a voluntary reporting system. Anyone, such as a parent, a health care provider, or friend of the patient, who suspects an association between a vaccination and an adverse event may report that event and information about it to VAERS. The CDC then investigates the event and tries to find out whether the adverse event was in fact caused by the vaccination.

The CDC states that they monitor VAERS data to:

- Detect new, unusual, or rare vaccine adverse events
- Monitor increases in known adverse events
- Identify potential patient risk factors for particular types of adverse events

- Identify vaccine lots with increased numbers or types of reported adverse events
- Assess the safety of newly licensed vaccines

Not all adverse events reported to VAERS are in fact caused by a vaccination. The two occurrences may be related in time only. And, it is probable that not all adverse events resulting from vaccination are reported to VAERS. The CDC states that many adverse events such as swelling at the injection site are underreported. Serious adverse events, according to the CDC, "are probably more likely to be reported than minor ones, especially when they occur soon after vaccination, even if they may be coincidental and related to other causes."

VAERS has successfully identified several rare adverse events related to vaccination. Among them are:

- An intestinal problem after the first vaccine for rotavirus was introduced (the vaccine was withdrawn in 1999)
- Neurologic and gastrointestinal diseases related to yellow fever vaccine

Additionally, according to Plotkin et al., VAERS identified a need for further investigation of MMR association with a blood clotting disorder, encephalopathy after MMR, and syncope after immunization (Plotkin SA et al. *Vaccines*, 5th ed. Philadelphia: Saunders, 2008).

Vaccine Safety Datalink

The CDC established this system in 1990. The VSD is a collection of linked databases containing information from large medical groups. The linked databases allow officials to gather data about vaccination among the populations served by the medical groups. Researchers can access the data by proposing studies to the CDC and having them approved.

The VSD has some drawbacks. For example, few completely unvaccinated children are listed in the database. The medical groups providing information to VSD may have patient populations that are not representative of large populations in general. Additionally, the data come not from randomized, controlled, blinded trials but from actual medical practice. Therefore, it may be difficult to control and evaluate the data.

Rapid Cycle Analysis is a program of the VSD, launched in 2005. It monitors real-time data to compare rates of adverse events in recently vaccinated people with rates among unvaccinated people. The system is used mainly to monitor new vaccines. Among the new vaccines being monitored in Rapid Cycle Analysis are the conjugated meningococcal vaccine, rotavirus vaccine, MMRV vaccine, Tdap vaccine, and the HPV vaccine. Possible associations between adverse events and vaccination are then studied further.

Vaccine Injury Compensation

For information on systems for compensating individuals who have been harmed by vaccines, see our article on Vaccine Injury Compensation Programs (https://www.historyofvaccines.org/content/articles/vaccine-injury-compensation-programs).

7

Measles Is Still a Deadly Disease

Paul Duprex

Dr. Paul Duprex is a professor of molecular genetics and microbiology at the University of Pittsburgh. Dr. Duprex is an expert on the mumps and measles viruses. He directs a biocontainment laboratory where scientists can safely conduct research on possibly deadly diseases.

Dr. Paul Duprex analyzes the serious situation surrounding measles both past and present. He outlines the case for education, continued vaccination, and enhanced surveillance around this disease. Dr. Duprex points out that before a vaccination was available, a huge number of people around the world died from the measles each year. Then when the vaccine became available, many parents in the US and Europe had their children vaccinated because they knew of the devastation caused by the disease. Interestingly, measles is making a comeback and causing problems. The doctor asserts that a lack of knowledge about the disease is causing parents who don't know better not to have their children vaccinated.

On the darkest day of 2018, the winter solstice, we at the Center for Vaccine Research at the University of Pittsburgh tweeted, with despair, a report in the *Guardian* that measles cases in Europe reached the highest number in 20 years.

Why was this a cause for concern? Europe is far away from the United States, and as some people apparently believe, measles is a

"Measles: Why It's So Deadly, and Why Vaccination Is So Vital," by Paul Duprex, The Conversation, February 1, 2019, https://theconversation.com/measles-why-its-so-deadly-and-why-vaccination-is-so-vital-110779. Licensed under CC BY ND 4.0 International.

benign, childhood disease that causes a bit of a rash, a dribbling nose and a few spots, right? What was all the fuss about?

Well as George Santayana said, "Those who cannot remember the past are condemned to repeat it." Collective amnesia about the virulence of this disease has driven us to forget that measles virus has killed tens of millions of infants throughout history. Now, with several ongoing outbreaks across our own country, this unnecessary threat is back.

Measles is a highly contagious and sometimes deadly disease that spreads like wildfire in naive populations. The virus played its part in decimating Native American populations during the age of discovery. Since these people groups had no natural immunity to the diseases brought to the New World by Europeans, some estimates suggest up to 95 percent of the Native American population died due to smallpox, measles and other infectious diseases.

In the 1960s, measles infected about 3-4 million people in the US each year. More than 48,000 people were hospitalized, and about 4,000 developed acute encephalitis, a life-threatening condition in which brain tissues become inflamed. Up to 500 people died, mainly from complications such as pneumonia and encephalitis. This was why vaccine pioneers John Enders and Thomas Peebles were motivated to isolate, weaken and develop a vaccine against measles that is truly transformative for human health. Parents who knew the reality of the disease were quick to vaccinate their children. Uptake skyrocketed and the number of cases, and associated deaths, plummeted in the developed world.

By 1985, when John Enders died, over 1 million of the world's kids were still dying because of this infection. However, now measles was a disease preventable by vaccine, and there was a huge impetus to address that tragedy by the World Health Organization.

When I started working on the virus in 1996, there were still over 500,000 children dying of measles each year worldwide. Such big numbers can be hard to digest. So to put it into perspective, if you've ever been on or seen a Boeing 747 jumbo jet, you will know it's a pretty big airplane. Think of over three of these planes full of infants crashing every day of the year with 100 percent of the people on board dying. January, February, March … the summer solstice, the autumnal equinox … November, back to the winter solstice in December … one rhythmic year. That's the reality of measles—over half-a-million lives were lost globally every year in the nineties.

Thanks to vaccination, however, between 2000 and 2016 there was an 84 percent decrease in measles mortality, and over 20 millions deaths were prevented due to vaccination. What an achievement!

Near universal adoption of the vaccine in the developing world meant that measles infections and concomitant deaths became very rare. By 2000, the vaccine led to measles being eliminated from the United States. The last person to die of the infection here was in 2015.

The Effectiveness and Irony of Vaccination

These successes don't mean the measles is gone or that the virus has become weak. Far from it. Seeing the virus up close and personal over all these years and knowing what happens when it runs rampant in an infected host gives me such respect for this minuscule "little bag of destruction" whose genetic material is 19,000 times smaller than ours. It's also ironic how losing sight of the disease because of the success of vaccination has brought new societal challenges.

What's important to realize is those millions of kids who died of measles each year in the nineties, for the most part were not living in the developed world. In those days here in the United States and in Europe, there was a widespread appreciation that vaccines work, meaning that the vast majority of people received the measles, mumps and rubella (MMR) vaccine and were well and truly protected. Two doses of the vaccine are 97 percent effective at stopping the infection.

What one of the most infectious pathogens on the planet can do to an unvaccinated person in 2019 is biologically incredible. Yes, that's right, an unvaccinated human. But why would anyone decide not to get vaccinated or refrain from protecting their children?

That's because forgetting the past has precipitated selective amnesia in our post-measles psyche. Ignoring scientific facts has tragically brought us to a place where some people fail to appreciate the values and utility of some of the most phenomenal tools we have created in our historical war on infectious disease. Unsubstantiated claims that vaccines like MMR were associated with autism, multiple sclerosis, Crohn's disease, etc., etc., and ill-informed celebrities have wreaked havoc with vaccination programs. Genuine, caring parents unaware of the realities of diseases they had never seen decided that since the viruses were gone from this part of the world shots were so last millennium. Put simply, some people have given up on vaccines.

This has created the perfect storm. Since the measles virus is so infectious and Europe, Africa, South America, and South East Asia are not really that far away by jumbo jet, a case somewhere in the world can lead to an infection anywhere in the world. Failure to vaccinate large groups of people is helping measles come back. From California to New York, from Washington state to Minnesota and Georgia, measles is back with a vengeance. Now we can only live in hope that the last death from this deadly disease in the US remains from 2015. Unfortunately, that is not a given.

8

Getting a Flu Shot Protects You and Those Around You

Brie Zeltner

Brie Zeltner is a journalist reporting for the Plain Dealer *in Cleveland, Ohio. She specializes in stories with a medical focus.*

Every year doctors and other health providers hear the same objections from people who do not get vaccinated against the flu. The health system says that two populations in the US generally get the vaccine—the young and the old. But more people need to be vaccinated, especially the people in between those ages. Why? Because when a great proportion of the population is protected against the virus this helps those individuals who for medical reasons cannot get the shot. Herd immunity works, as shown in this viewpoint.

Most people who skip the flu shot every year have a long list of reasons for doing so: I never get the flu; the flu isn't dangerous; the vaccination gives you the flu; I'm not likely to get very sick from the flu if I'm infected.

Of all these reasons, only the last is true—and only for a certain group of people. For healthy young adults, it is unlikely that the flu will be deadly or dangerous enough to require hospitalization. So why is it important, then, that everyone get the shot?

The best answer might be herd immunity, which is what immunologists define as the protection of the weak and vulnerable

"Flu and Herd Immunity: Getting the Shot Is as Important for the Community as for You," by Brie Zeltner, Advance Ohio, October 23, 2012. Reprinted by permission.

that arises when enough of the population is vaccinated to shield them from infection.

Of course, vaccinating yourself vastly increases the odds that you won't get sick with flu this season, but it also protects everyone you come into contact with: your parents, your sister's new baby, the stranger on the bus who can't get vaccinated because of an egg allergy, and everyone who isn't able to weather an infection as well as you.

The idea of herd immunity is like a moat around a castle or the natural behavior of herd animals when threatened by a predator. The strong surround the weak to protect them from attack; in this case the vaccinated protect those who can't be vaccinated or those with low immunity from contact with the flu by halting the spread of the virus.

"Herd immunity is the idea that if I'm the one cow who can't get vaccinated surrounded by all the other cows who did, then they can't give me anything," says Cindy Modie, supervisor of vaccine services at the Cuyahoga County Board of Health. "So I'm safe as long as I'm in the middle of the herd."

Depending on the illness in question, research has shown that it takes 80 percent to 95 percent vaccination coverage in a community to reach herd immunity. Diseases that are more easily spread, or that remain contagious for a longer period of time, usually require higher vaccination rates to keep them in check, Modie says.

Once Deadly, Now Rare

Herd immunity has been achieved in a lot of childhood illnesses that used to kill or disable, and that now are exceedingly rare in this country, says Dr. Alfred Connors, chief medical officer at MetroHealth Medical Center.

"We've done a very good job of vaccinating people against polio, pertussis [whooping cough], all of these illnesses that used to be the scourge of childhood," he says.

Diseases such as measles, mumps, pertussis and polio make headlines now only when herd immunity breaks down and children are again left vulnerable. Outbreaks of whooping cough have killed children in the past two years in California and other states where vaccination rates in small pockets of the population have dipped far below the national average.

Global travel also has widened the concept of "community" so much that "you now have to pay attention to the vaccine rate in the whole world," says Dr. Frank Esper, a pediatric infectious-disease specialist at University Hospitals Rainbow Babies & Children's Hospital.

This is why he and his colleagues watch the spread of polio in certain areas of the world.

"Why should I care about polio in Afghanistan?" he asks. "There are plenty of people moving to and from Afghanistan right now, and the disease is going to come back if we don't keep up our end of the bargain in keeping our children vaccinated."

"We're no longer that isolated cow that can stay amongst the vaccinated herd, because of travel," says Modie.

Still, high vaccination rates act as a buffer if a virus does enter from the outside, she says. This was the case last year during the largest outbreak of measles in the US in 15 years, which public health officials believe was triggered by cases among people who were infected while traveling mostly to Western Europe.

The outbreak, which affected more than 200 children, could have been much worse. More than half the cases were among people who were eligible for the vaccine but not vaccinated. The spread was contained, and there were no deaths.

"Bobbing and Weaving" with the Flu Bug

Vaccinating the "herd" at a high enough level to protect the most vulnerable is a particular challenge with the flu.

It's been easier to achieve herd immunity with diseases such as measles and chicken pox because the vaccines that prevent these childhood illnesses are much longer acting, explains Esper.

When you need only a single shot, or a booster several years later, people tend to be more willing to comply with a vaccination, he says.

Because the flu virus is constantly adapting to the antibodies the immune system produces, we need a new vaccine each season to combat it.

"Unfortunately the virus' strategy of how to infect people is to change itself over and over and over again to kind of bob and weave its way through the antibodies, so that none of them works so well," says Esper. "We always have to keep up with the changes of the virus."

Reluctance to get a shot every year is part of the reason why national flu vaccination rates are so dismal—about 40 percent of the country each year—far below the 80 percent to 90 percent needed to achieve herd immunity and protect the most vulnerable in the population.

"We're pretty bad when it comes to flu vaccination," says Esper.

For certain groups, namely those between the ages of 18 and 49, the rate is even lower—about 29 percent, says Modie.

Ohio vaccination rates for polio and the MMR (measles, mumps and rubella) vaccines were about 94 percent in 2010, by comparison, according to the Ohio Department of Health.

In the past, the Centers for Disease Control and Prevention focused on flu vaccinations for high-risk groups. These include children under the age of 5, adults 65 and older, pregnant women and people with weakened immune systems or medical conditions such as asthma and lung disease that put them at higher risk of complications from the virus.

As a result, vaccination rates have reached almost 75 percent in the youngest children (6 to 23 months) and 65 percent in adults over the age of 65.

"If you get a high proportion of these people vaccinated, which we do a pretty good job of, then we can protect them," says Connors.

Still, not everyone can be vaccinated. Children under 6 months are too young and are dependent on immunity from their mothers. People who are allergic to eggs can't get the flu vaccine because the virus is grown inside a chicken egg. That makes it possible for traces of egg protein to remain in the vaccine and later trigger a reaction. People with a history of Guillain-Barre syndrome, a rare autoimmune disorder that causes nerve inflammation and muscle weakness, should also not be vaccinated because the illness can be triggered by the shot.

"Those are the people who are truly dependent on herd immunity, on everyone around them who can get the vaccine, to get vaccinated," Esper says.

And every year, people still die of complications related to the flu, mainly from pneumonia. These are primarily the very young and the very old, and people who have underlying illnesses that make it harder for them to recover from an infection, even if they are vaccinated. Influenza has killed between 3,000 and 49,000 people a year over the past 30 years, according to the CDC. The wide range reflects the variability and unpredictability of the illness.

In 2010, the CDC's Advisory Committee on Immunization Practices recommended universal vaccination for the first time, partly in reaction to the 2009 H1N1 pandemic flu virus, which hit young people particularly hard.

Vaccination rates have not risen appreciably since then.

The biggest barriers are myths about the flu shot that are as tenacious as the virus itself, the doctors say.

Every year, they fend them off with these reminders:

- The flu shot does not give you the flu. (Though it might make you feel a little under the weather for a while.)
- No one is naturally immune to the flu. (In fact, 20 percent of the population comes down with the illness every season, making it statistically certain that we'll all be infected at some point.)

- The flu shot is effective. (But not 100 percent of the time—nothing in medicine is perfect.)

"These [myths] are like urban legends," Esper says. "There's a lot of misinformation out there."

So is it possible to achieve herd immunity for seasonal flu? The experts say yes, though it would certainly be difficult.

"I wouldn't say that we're going to take it down to zero," Esper says. "But what we're trying to do is keep the score really, really low."

"If you were able to get 90 percent of the population vaccinated, it would be hard for influenza to take hold in the community," Connors says.

So as we enter flu season and you find yourself thinking you're invincible, or the shot is worthless, maybe it's time to think about everyone around you.

"If you get the flu vaccine, you're not getting it so much to protect yourself as to protect others," Connors says.

The wisdom of the herd, if you will.

9

Mandatory Vaccinations Are Incompatible with Liberty

Robert P. Murphy

Robert P. Murphy is senior economist at the Independent Energy Institute, a research assistant professor with the Free Market Institute at Texas Tech University, and a research fellow at the Independent Institute.

Which is more important: liberty of the individual or a collective good of public safety? That is the question addressed in the following viewpoint. When it comes to mandatory vaccines, the author argues, the answer is clear. Americans should not be forced to allow the state to inject substances into anyone's body against their will. The author goes a step further and views this issue through a libertarian lens, concluding that the question is not so complicated after all.

M andatory vaccinations are a gross violation of liberty. On some government policy issues—including mandatory quarantines, airport checkpoints, and NSA email scanning—there is at least a coherent allegation of a trade-off between individual freedom and public safety. But when it comes to mandatory vaccinations, there is little scope for plausible debate.

Mandatory vaccinations involve a supreme violation of liberty, where agents of the state inject substances into someone's body against his or her will. On the other side of the ledger, even in principle, mandatory vaccinations do not offer much benefit in enhanced public welfare, relative to a free society. When we throw in the realistic worries of government incompetence and malfeasance, the case against mandatory vaccinations is overwhelming.

Before making my case, I will explain in basic terms how different groups are likely to treat the proposition, according to major conceptions of the state's proper role. I do this in order to show that, even if we're being charitable to the most inclusive conceptions of liberty as a principle, mandatory vaccinations are still not justifiable.

First, among those who hew strictly to a nonaggression principle and a stateless society, mandatory vaccinations are, of course, a nonstarter. Whether they identify themselves as "strict libertarians," "voluntaryists," or "anarchocapitalists," this group would obviously never condone the state's forcing someone to be vaccinated, because most believe the state is illegitimate.

Second, for minarchists, the proper role for the state is that of a "night watchman," a minimal government that only protects the individual from domestic criminals and foreign threats. In a minarchist framework, it is only legitimate for the state to take action against someone who is violating (or threatening to violate) the rights of another. A person's failure to become vaccinated is hardly by itself a violation of someone else's rights. Flipping it around, it would sound odd to say you have the right to live in a society where everyone else has had measles shots.

Third, and most interesting, let's consider a broader notion of liberty, which balances a presumption of individual autonomy against the public welfare. In this approach, there's not a blanket prohibition on the state restricting the liberties of individuals— even when they haven't yet hurt anybody else—so long as such restrictions impose little harm on the recipients and possibly prevent a vast amount of damage. This is the only conception of the state for which the mandatory vaccination debate is possible.

Let's be charitable and assume this more expansive definition, under which, for example, even self-described libertarians might not object to stiff penalties for drunk driving or prohibitions on citizens building atomic bombs in their basements. How does mandatory vaccination fare in this framework, where we're not arguing in terms of qualitative principles but instead performing a quantitative cost-benefit test?

Even here, the case for mandatory vaccinations is weak. First of all, the only realistic scenario where the issue would even be relevant is where the vast majority of the public thinks it would be a good idea if everyone got vaccinated, but (for whatever reason) a small minority strongly disagreed. This is obvious: if the medical case for a vaccine were so dubious that, say, half the public didn't think it made sense to administer it, then there would hardly be an issue of the government clamoring to inject half the population against their will.

Now, let's push our analysis further. We're dealing with a scenario in which the vast majority of the public thinks it would be a good idea for all of the public to become vaccinated. In that environment, if vaccines are voluntary, then we can be confident that just about all of these enthusiasts would go ahead and become vaccinated. In other words, any "free riding" would only take place at the margin, if most of the population had gotten the vaccine and thus an outbreak of the relevant disease was unlikely.

This is a crucial point, and it shows why the case for mandatory vaccines is so much weaker than, for example, the case for mandatory restrictions on carbon dioxide emissions or mandatory contributions to the national military. When a person gets vaccinated, the primary beneficiary is himself. And this benefit is all the greater the lower the rate of vaccination in the population at large. In other words, among a population of people who all believe that a vaccine is effective, the individual cost-benefit analysis of taking the vaccine will only yield a temptation of "free riding" once a sufficient fraction of the population has become vaccinated, thus ensuring "herd immunity."

Unlike other examples of huge (alleged) trade-offs between individual and public benefits, with vaccinations there is no threat of a mass outbreak in a free society. With vaccines, we have the happy outcome that when someone chooses to vaccinate him or herself, so long as the vaccine is effective, then that person is largely shielded from the consequences of others' decisions regarding vaccination.

However, the proponents of mandatory vaccinations say that this analysis is too glib. There are people who can't undergo certain vaccinations because of medical conditions, including young people (babies) who are not yet old enough to receive certain shots. It is to protect these vulnerable pockets of the population that some want the state to force vaccinations on those who are too ignorant or too selfish to recognize their duty of living in a community.

Notice the irony and how weak the mandatory vaccination case has become. We are no longer being told that vaccines are "safe," and that anyone who fears medical complications is a conspiracy theorist trusting Jenny McCarthy over guys in white lab coats. On the contrary, the CDC warns certain groups not to take popular vaccines because of the health risks. This is no longer a matter of principle—of the people on the side of science being pro-vaccine, while the tinfoil-hatters are anti-vaccine. Instead it's a disagreement over which people should be taking the vaccine and which people should not take it because the dangers are too great.

Regarding children, social conflict can be resolved through the fuller application of private property rights. If all schools, hospitals, and daycare centers were privately operated and had the legal right to exclude whichever clients they wished, then the owners could decide on vaccination policies. Any parents who were horrified at the idea of little Jimmy playing with an unvaccinated kid could choose Jimmy's school accordingly.

We have seen that even assuming the best of government officials, it is difficult to state an argument in favor of mandatory vaccinations. Yet, the debate tilts even more when we recall that throughout history, government officials have made horrible decisions in the name of public welfare, either through incompetence or ulterior motives. It should be obvious that no fan of liberty can support injecting substances into an innocent person's body against his or her will.

10

Vaccinations Cannot Be Forced

Bretigne Shaffer

Bretigne Shaffer is a journalist, independent writer, and author who worked as a journalist in Asia for many years. She blogs at On the Banks.

In the following viewpoint, Bretigne Shaffer argues that herd immunity is essentially a lie forced upon people by drug companies and others to convince people to be vaccinated. She argues that people have no right to expect others to comply with generally accepted ideas and wisdom from others. Shaffer maintains that this is a libertarian concept—you may protect yourself and those close to you, but you may not force others to do so.

It's hard to think of a more fundamental right than the right to determine what happens to one's own body. Forcing someone to undergo medical treatment against their will violates this most basic of rights—the right to be free from physical assault. Yet even some libertarians have jumped on the mandatory vaccination bandwagon, arguing that one person not taking every possible precaution against contracting a disease constitutes an assault against another. But this line of thinking requires some very tortured logic.

"Libertarians for Forced Vaccinations?" by Bretigne Shaffer, Foundation for Economic Education, March 26, 2019, https://fee.org/articles/libertarians-for-forced-vaccinations/. Licensed under CC BY 4.0 International.

What Rights?

To begin with, nobody has a "right" to a germ-free environment outside of their own property (and good luck establishing one there). Proponents of vaccine mandates assert this "right" as if it is a long-standing social or legal norm, but it is not. Human beings have been living among each other for millennia, and there has never been a widely asserted right to freedom from any and all pathogens at others' expense.

There has, historically, been a widely held and asserted expectation of quarantine in the case of exceptionally dangerous illnesses. However, this is not at all what the proponents of mandated vaccines are calling for. Quarantine is simply the demand that those who are already infected with a disease remain isolated in their homes or elsewhere until they are no longer able to infect others.

This is profoundly different from what the pro-mandate crowd demands: that those who are not infected undergo a medical procedure to minimize their chances of becoming infected. This is a much more intrusive demand and a potentially dangerous one.

Seriously? Measles?

Furthermore, measles—the scariest thing the mandate pushers can come up with—is not even on the list of federally quarantinable diseases. And rightly so, as it hardly qualifies as an exceptionally dangerous disease in the developed world.

Long before the vaccine was available, the mortality rate had fallen to around 1 in 10,000 cases, and it was widely considered to be a benign childhood illness that nearly everyone contracted.

So what has changed in the last few years? How is it that all of a sudden, measles has gone from a disease not even worthy of mandatory quarantine for the infected to one that has generated near-mass hysteria and demands for the far more intrusive forced medical intervention against those who are not infected?

What About Herd Immunity?

In 2016, then-Libertarian presidential candidate Gary Johnson announced that he had reversed his position on vaccine mandates and now supported them. The reason? Someone told him about herd immunity:

> ...I've come to find out that without mandatory vaccines, the vaccines that would in fact be issued would not be effective. So ... it's dependent that you have mandatory vaccines so that every child is immune. Otherwise, not all children will be immune even though they receive a vaccine.

Had Johnson looked just a little more deeply, he would have learned that the theory of vaccine-induced herd immunity is not as solid as its proponents would have us believe. The idea was first put forward by A.W. Hedrich in 1933, based on his observation that measles outbreaks were suppressed when 68 percent of children had contracted the measles virus. This observation had nothing to do with vaccination, as the measles vaccine had not even been developed yet.

This is an important distinction for a few reasons. Perhaps most importantly: While the immunity conferred by contracting measles lasts a lifetime, that conferred by vaccination does not. What this means is that a 90 percent vaccination rate does not equate to 90 percent of the population having immunity. As Dr. Russell Blaylock says:

> It was not until relatively recently that it was discovered that most of these vaccines lost their effectiveness 2 to 10 years after being given. What this means is that at least half the population, that is the baby boomers, have had no vaccine-induced immunity against any of these diseases for which they had been vaccinated very early in life. In essence, at least 50% or more of the population was unprotected for decades.
>
> If we listen to present-day wisdom, we are all at risk of resurgent massive epidemics should the vaccination rate fall below 95%. Yet, we have all lived for at least 30 to 40 years with 50% or less of the population having vaccine protection. That is,

> *herd immunity has not existed in this country for many decades and no resurgent epidemics have occurred. Vaccine-induced herd immunity is a lie used to frighten doctors, public-health officials, other medical personnel, and the public into accepting vaccinations.*

The larger point, though, is that even if the idea of vaccine-induced herd immunity did hold up to scrutiny, it would at best be a positive externality—not something that anyone has the right to demand from others at gunpoint.

But What About Those Who Cannot Be Vaccinated?

Others have written more comprehensively on the fallacy of using medically fragile people as an excuse for forcing everyone to be vaccinated. So I'll just say this: Nobody has an obligation to vaccinate themselves or their children in order to protect the most medically vulnerable among us.

My own daughter is intellectually disabled and suffers from seizures. Much of the outside world is a dangerous and scary place where she could easily be badly hurt or worse. Yet I would never dream of using force to compel those around me to make the world safe for my daughter. Keeping her safe is my job and my husband's job—not everyone else's.

I doubt that those who promote this line of thinking have really thought through the implications of what they are asking for: requiring everyone to alter their lives and actions in order to accommodate the most medically fragile, at all times and in all spaces. What they are demanding has implications far beyond vaccines.

Adults Too?

And if they really do believe that not being vaccinated constitutes a form of aggression against others, then why confine their demands to children?

Why should you and I and the vast majority of all adults in the US be exempt from the requirement to be completely up to date on all of the vaccines the CDC and its pharmaceutical industry cronies have decided we should have? Are we not also committing aggression every day we go out in public, exposing others to diseases we do not yet have but might possibly contract?

Of course, if disease transmission is really what the proponents of vaccine mandates are worried about, then they should also demand that those recently vaccinated with live-virus vaccines not be allowed in schools or any public spaces. And if they aren't demanding this, then one has to wonder whether the transmission of disease really is their primary concern.

The bottom line, though, has nothing to do with the science behind vaccines, nor with herd immunity, nor competing claims about vaccine safety and vaccine harm. Nor does it have to do with how serious diseases like measles are or are not. It is simply this: You do not have the right to force a medical procedure on another person.

This is libertarian thinking 101. You are free to do whatever you wish with what is yours—and other people are not yours. You do not own them, and you do not get to make decisions over their bodies and their lives. You may exclude them from your property if you wish, but you may not force them to undergo medical (or non-medical) procedures against their will. You don't even have to be a libertarian to understand this. The right to bodily integrity, to be free from assault, is the most fundamental of all human rights. If it is not protected, then no other rights even matter.

11

Overconfident People Don't Believe Experts About Vaccines

Matthew Motta, Steven Sylvester, and Timothy Callaghan

Matthew Motta is a postdoctoral fellow in science communication at the Annenberg Public Policy Center. Steven Sylvester is an assistant professor at Utah Valley University specializing in public policy. Dr. Timothy Callaghan is an assistant professor at Texas A & M University School of Public Health.

In the following viewpoint, Matthew Motta, Steven Sylvester, and Timothy Callaghan make and support an interesting point of contention about those not supporting vaccination. The Dunning-Kruger effect demonstrates that too many Americans believe they know as much or more about medical and scientific principles than professionals in those fields. Celebrities and politicians make it even harder for professionals to end the myths surrounding vaccination.

One of the most contentious areas of health policy over the past two decades has been the safety of vaccination. Vaccines prevent the outbreak of diseases that used to be widespread, like polio, and scientific consensus strongly supports their safety. Yet many Americans refuse or delay the vaccination of their children out of fear that it could lead to autism, even though scientific consensus refutes this claim.

Anti-vaccine attitudes have been fueled in large part by growing rates of autism diagnoses as well as a now debunked study in the *Lancet* that linked autism and the measles mumps rubella (MMR) vaccine—pushing many parents to see vaccination as a potential explanation for their child's autism diagnosis.

The growing "anti-vax" movement here and abroad has seen parents refuse to give their children mandatory school vaccinations, growing numbers of celebrities questioning vaccine safety, and even pet owners refusing to vaccinate their dogs—forcing the British Veterinary Association to issue a statement in April that dogs cannot develop autism.

Given the consistent message from the scientific community about the safety of vaccines, and evidence of vaccine success as seen through the eradication of diseases, why has the skepticism about vaccines continued?

One possibility is that attitudes about medical experts help to explain the endorsement of anti-vax attitudes. Specifically, building on past research, our research team contends that some US adults might support anti-vax policy positions in part because they believe they know more than medical experts about autism and its causes. We wanted to test this theory.

Vaccine Skepticism and Knowledge

Vaccination has been one of public health's greatest success stories. It led to the eradication of smallpox and to widespread elimination of polio. Eradication of a disease means that it has been permanently wiped out and that intervention efforts are no longer necessary; smallpox so far is the only disease that has been eradicated. Elimination means a reduction to zero incidence in a specific geographic area as a result of deliberate efforts. Vaccination has protected millions from the ravages of tetanus, whooping cough and even chicken pox.

And yet, vaccine skepticism persists, extending into the political realm, with many politicians questioning the safety of vaccines. Most notably, President Donald Trump has questioned the credentials of doctors calling for vaccination, pushed for slowed vaccination schedules, and tapped vaccine skeptic Robert Kennedy Jr. to chair an administrative panel on vaccine safety.

We wondered: Could the inability of anti-vaxxers to accurately appraise their own knowledge and skills compared to those of medical experts play a role in shaping their attitudes about vaccines? This inability to accurately appraise one's own knowledge is called the Dunning-Kruger effect, first identified in social psychology. Dunning-Kruger effects occur when individuals' lack of knowledge about a particular subject leads them to inaccurately gauge their expertise on that subject. Ignorance of one's own ignorance can lead people who lack knowledge on a subject to think of themselves as more expert than those who are comparatively better informed. We refer to this as "overconfidence."

Dunning-Kruger Effects and Anti-Vax Attitudes

To test our hypothesis, our research asked more than 1,300 Americans in December 2017 to compare their own perceived levels of knowledge about the causes of autism to those of medical doctors and scientists. After doing that, we asked respondents to answer a series of factual knowledge questions about autism, as well as the extent to which they agree with misinformation about a potential link between childhood vaccines and autism.

We found that 34 percent of US adults in our sample feel that they know as much or more than scientists about the causes of autism. Slightly more, or 36 percent, feel the same way about their knowledge relative to that of medical doctors.

We also found strong evidence of Dunning-Kruger effects in our sample. Sixty-two percent of those who performed worst on our autism knowledge test believe that they know as much or more than both doctors and scientists about the causes of autism, compared to only 15 percent of those scoring best on the knowledge test. Likewise, 71 percent of those who strongly endorse misinformation about the link between vaccines and autism feel that they know as much or more than medical doctors about the causes of autism, compared to only 28 percent of those who most strongly reject that misinformation.

We recently published our findings at the journal *Social Science and Medicine*.

How Does This Affect Vaccine Policy?

Our research also finds that these Dunning-Kruger effects have important implications for vaccine policy.

In addition to gauging autism knowledge, our survey asked respondents to share their opinions on several aspects of vaccine policy. For example, we asked respondents whether or not they support parents' decisions to not vaccinate their children before sending them to public schools. Respondents could tell us whether they strongly agree, agree, neither agree nor disagree, disagree or strongly disagree with that statement.

We found that nearly a third, or 30 percent, of people who think that they know more than medical experts about the causes of autism strongly support giving parents the latitude to not vaccinate their children. In contrast, 16 percent of those who do not think that they know more than medical professionals felt the same way.

Our study also finds that people who think they know more than medical experts are more likely to trust information about vaccines from non-expert sources, such as celebrities. These individuals are also more likely to support a strong role for non-experts in the process of making policies that pertain to vaccines and vaccination.

An Uphill Battle?

Ultimately, our results point to the uphill battle that the scientific community faces as it confronts growing anti-vax sentiment from the public and politicians alike. Even as the mountain of evidence on the safety and importance of vaccines from doctors and scientists continues to grow, many Americans think they know more than the experts trying to correct their misperceptions.

Therefore, finding new ways to present scientific consensus on vaccines to an audience skeptical of medical experts should be a priority. Our research suggests that one interesting area for future research could be to examine whether pro-vaccine information from non-expert sources like celebrities could persuade those with anti-vaccine policy attitudes to change their minds.

12

Why Has Mistrust of Vaccinations and Other Science Taken Hold?

Zoe Williams

Zoe Williams is a journalist and author who works as a columnist for the Guardian.

In the following viewpoint, Zoe Williams presents an issue worthy of reflection. Why has a mistrust of what is scientifically proven gaining a foothold, especially in the United States? Williams points out that at one time anti-vaxxer conspiracy beliefs were part of the hippie counterculture. What can explain this, and how can prominent US Republicans be part of this anti-science, anti-evidence movement?

Half of all parents have seen anti-vaccination messages on social media, according to a report from the Royal Society for Public Health. It's not all bad news: 90% of parents still have the sense to get their children vaccinated, whatever they read, just as almost all Mumsnet users stay in secure family units rather than moving to all-female communes, despite the proliferation of fake news on the site about what husbands are like.

Yet, of course, this is serious: measles—upon which the anti-vaxxer conspiracy so often alights—requires 90-95% of the population to be immune in order for the inoculation to hold. This is only true of contagious diseases. If the anti-vaxxers concentrated on spreading nonsense about the tetanus jab, they would do no

"Anti-Vaxxers Are Thriving—Because We Live in a Fact-Phobic Wild West," by Zoe Williams, Guardian News and Media Limited, January 25, 2019. Reprinted by permission.

harm to anyone but themselves and their own children. But where would be the fun in that? They have surprisingly little to say on this soil-transmitted disease.

So we're already scraping the floor of public safety, for no better reason than that a wild conspiracy theory that in another age would have been discredited, bringing down with it one, maybe two reputations, got lucky with a networked age and a global culture war. It is a classic hot-button issue, combining—on the pro-vaccine side—the elegance and rigour of evidence-based science, with the white-hot primal rage of parental protectiveness.

Yet the roots of the anti-vax movement are telling. Like so much that is attached to parenting, and specifically motherhood, the movement is a highly significant cultural development that is siloed and, broadly speaking, ignored until some tragedy happens. I believe this is on the specious grounds that parenting is apolitical— or more precisely, nothing a mother could think or do could ever have wider contextual meaning. As a parable, but also, a truth, you can write a book about the culture of parenting, and it'll get stuck in the health section, and nobody will ever notice or read it except by accident, when they will find it has very little information on health.

To distrust medicine, or to give it its archaic name, "western medicine," was once the preserve of the hippy left. In the early days of the anti-vax movement, at the turn of this century, those who distrusted vaccinations spanned the political spectrum. Only in the past decade has it become the drum beat of the American right, and it's only in the past few years that prominent Republicans— Chris Christie and Rand Paul in 2015—took it on as a rallying cry. How an issue gets from US campaign literature to a Facebook page in Hebden Bridge is hard to pinpoint; suffice it to say that, from Islamophobia to cases such as baby Charlie Gard's, we know that it happens.

It dovetails with a generalised anti-science movement: climate-change denial, scorn for any epidemiological data about inequality and its effects, a generalised repudiation of expertise. We tend to look at each trend individually, and through the wrong end of the telescope. Climate-change deniers are funded by the fossil-fuel industry; free market fundamentalists also, conveniently, run hedge funds. And these tawdry explanations seem to make sense but miss the point: it's not narrow self-interest that drives the fightback against evidence, but rather, an entire worldview.

Scientific discovery tends towards the collective: it takes the hive mind to produce it, and the answers it provides tend to be socially located: vaccinate; redistribute; recycle. Science is levelling and pluralistic: it situates authority not with any one person or type of person, but in the disembodied, infinitely accessible space of evidence. Whether it's a measles jab or a climate model, the far right hates it. Furthermore, when facts have been contested so energetically as to have been effectively obliterated from the terrain, all that is left is feeling; power is restored to the person who feels the most strongly, where that person always believed it belonged.

The question is, how did this ideological crankery find an audience? Why haven't people been more resilient, more wedded to the world of the evidence-base? Here the contexts peel apart: climate-change denial is a lot more comforting to believe than climate-change evidence. In parenting, the established authorities, whether the World Trade Organization or the NHS, have become defined by such caution (don't sit on new furniture, formula milk gives you cancer) that a wild west mentality has taken over.

Experts, after a decade or so of over-statement, have undermined themselves, and everything has to be double-checked on Facebook. Yet the root solution is the same: somehow the credibility of evidence has to radically renew itself; an epidemic of measles may be the most dramatic risk, otherwise, but it will be only the end of a tangled skein.

13

Why Parents Refuse Childhood Vaccination

Irene A. Harmsen, et al.

Irene A. Harmsen is affiliated with the National Institute for Public Health and the Environment (RIVM), Centre for Infectious Disease Control, the Netherlands, and the Department of Work & Social Psychology, Maastricht University, the Netherlands.

Recent measles outbreaks in the United States have revealed that more parents have chosen to not vaccinate their children than was previously thought. But this is not a problem that is confined to the United States. Despite the success of vaccine-prevention programs in the Netherlands and other high-income countries, many parents question—and some refuse—vaccination for their children. The following study attempts to qualify the factors behind these decisions. The researchers found that public health information was not sufficient for these parents, and indeed a lack of trust in public health systems was a factor in undercutting recommendations for vaccination.

In recent decades, vaccine-preventable diseases have been greatly reduced through routine vaccination programs in high income countries. In The Netherlands, the National Immunization Program (NIP) is a voluntary program that offers childhood

"Why Parents Refuse Childhood Vaccination: A Qualitative Study Using Online Focus Groups," by Irene A. Harmsen, Liesbeth Mollema, Robert AC Ruiter, Theo G.W. Paulussen, Hester E. de Melker, and Gerjo Kok, BMC Public Health 2013 13:1183, December 16, 2013, https://bmcpublichealth.biomedcentral.com /articles/10.1186/1471-2458-13-1183. Licensed under CC BY 2.0.

vaccinations free of charge and includes vaccines against twelve infectious diseases (i.e., polio, diphtheria, tetanus, pertussis, rubella, measles, mumps, disease caused by Haemophilus influenzae type b, meningococcal C disease, hepatitis B, pneumococcal disease and cervical cancer caused by human papillomavirus (HPV)). Children aged 0–4 years receive the vaccines at child welfare centres (CWC), where they also get free-of-charge health check-ups during consults attended alternately by physicians and nurses on a scheduled basis. Parents can choose between a regular CWC or a CWC based on anthroposophy, a spiritual philosophy founded by Rudolf Steiner. The Dutch Health Council recommends the vaccines included in the NIP, and the National Institute of Public Health and the Environment (RIVM) manages the program implementations of the NIP and provides parents and health care workers with information about vaccinations. Parents of infants receive some oral information about the NIP when a nurse of the CWC visits the parents at their home in the first week after birth of their infant. After that (when the child is 4–6 weeks old), parents receive a brochure with information about vaccines, (vaccine-preventable) diseases, vaccination schedules, and side effects.

Overall, vaccination coverage in The Netherlands is 95% (except for HPV). Despite the success of the NIP, many parents appeared to become more critical about childhood vaccination in the last few years, at least as far as HPV-vaccination is concerned. In The Netherlands, there was a wide debate in the national press about the 2009 introduction of vaccination for HPV for 12 year old girls, resulting in mixed messages and confused feelings in the population. The expected HPV vaccination coverage of 70% turned out to be about 50%. Also, at the end of 2009, during the H1N1 influenza pandemic, Dutch parents criticized the quality of information about the risks and benefits of the influenza vaccination, which was provided by the national health authorities. A well-known group who refuse vaccination are conservative Protestants living in what is called the Bible Belt region, which stretches from the southwest to the northeast of the country.

Such refusals have been influenced by tradition or predominantly religious arguments. Parents who refuse vaccinations might also be influenced by other factors.

Refusal of childhood vaccination may be influenced by concerns about vaccine components, low perceived likelihood and severity of the infectious diseases, and a trusting relationship with a natural healer or another respected person who doubts vaccination safety and effectiveness, Hilton et al. showed that some parents fear an overload of the immune system caused by combination vaccines. Additionally, the perception that vaccination is more risky than non-immunization and issues of harm, distrust and access might play a role in refusing childhood vaccination. According to Sporton et al., parents who refused vaccination made a well-considered decision based on an assessment of the benefits and the risks of vaccination, the child's susceptibility to the potential disease, and the acceptance of responsibility for that decision.

The aim of this study is to attain more insight into these factors in order to design public information and interventions that will help parents make decisions that best serve their children and the wider community. We performed internet-based focus groups with parents who had refused all or part of the NIP recommendations for children 0–4 years old.

Methods

The focus group discussions were conducted online because the diverse population was difficult to reach and lived throughout The Netherlands, making face-to-face focus groups infeasible. Online focus groups are used more and more, in part because participants can choose their own time to answer questions. Moreover, costs and time can be saved through the automatic and accurate storing of discussion data. The focus group method in general is effective for exploring people's opinions and experiences. The group process can help individuals to clarify their views that might not emerge from a one-on-one interview.

Study Participants

Study participants were randomly selected from Praeventis, the vaccination database in The Netherlands. Participants were selected based on the vaccination status of their children (0–4 years old). Postal codes were used to exclude residents of the Bible Belt, whose reasons for refusing vaccinations have been explored by others. We invited 250 parents with partially vaccinated children (PV parents) and 250 parents with children not vaccinated at all (NV parents). We defined children (aged 0–4 years) as partially vaccinated when they missed one or more NIP vaccinations, and as not vaccinated when they missed all vaccinations in the program.

Procedure

Parents received a letter containing information about the study and a reply form to complete and return if they wanted to participate. Those opting to participate received an e-mail with information about the use of the online focus groups and a personal log-in name and password, by which they could anonymously access the online forum. When participants responded to each topic discussed by the online group they received a gift voucher of €30 as an incentive. Of the researchers, only the moderator and assistant had access to the forum, for collecting the data. Anonymity of statements in the transcripts and in the final report was ensured, as was confidentially of the data. Because data collection was through the Internet, participants gave informed consent by clicking a button after having read all relevant information. The study was approved by Maastricht University's Ethics Committee of Psychology.

Study Setting

The focus groups were based on a semi-structured protocol with open-ended questions and minimal control, allowing participants to discuss all aspects of each posting. The list of topics was developed beforehand, in consultation with all the authors, and subsequently tested with other colleagues who had young children. Each of the online focus groups was conducted over 5 days during one week. The focus groups ran during November and December

2011. The forum was accessible only to parents who had responded to the invitation letter and received a log-in name and password. Each week, Monday through Friday, the moderator posted a new topic at the forum daily, and the group participants were alerted by e-mail. All postings remained open for response throughout the week. The focus groups were asynchronic, which means that participants were free to log into the forum discussions at any time to read all postings and respond within one week. The moderator regularly checked the forum and, when necessary, asked additional questions to clarify comments of participants. The content and format of postings were identical for all focus groups.

The forum for each group started with an introduction and with questions for participants about their family composition, the CWC that they visited, and perceived positive and negative aspects of the NIP. On the second day, parents were asked which factors influenced their decision to refuse any or all vaccinations. On the third day, they were asked about their need for NIP information. The fourth day focused on their perceptions about new vaccines within the NIP. The fifth day was used to end the discussion, with an evaluation of the focus group by the participants. After conducting 8 sets of focus groups, analysis indicated that data saturation had been reached, making the inclusion of more respondents unnecessary.

Analysis

The data was analyzed based on a thematic analysis performed to explore factors that influenced parents' decision to refuse vaccination. The main themes of the data were based on the topics and questions posted at the online forum. An inductive process was used to code and analyze the data for the sub-themes from these main themes. The data was analyzed and coded by the moderator. An independent researcher analyzed a sample of the data; afterwards the initial coding was compared, reviewed, discussed, and refined until consensus could be achieved, which led to a more representative coding scheme and criteria. Using software program NVivo 9 (QSR International), separate analyses were conducted for PV parents and NV parents.

Results

Participants

In total, we held 8 one-week online focus groups with all the parents who responded to the invitation (n = 60) and who had refused all or part of NIP vaccinations on non-religious grounds. Of the 8 groups, 5 included parents who completely refused vaccinations (n = 39, 7–9 parents each), and 3 included parents who partially refused vaccinations (n = 21, 7 parents each).

Five parents had one child; most parents had two (n = 34) or three children (n = 14); 6 parents had four children, and one parent had five children. Most parents visited a regular CWC (NV = 25, PV = 19), some parents visited an anthroposophical CWC (NV = 10, PV = 1), and some parents used no CWC at all (NV = 4, PV = 1). Because of the anonymity of the participants, no other demographic variables (like gender) were available.

The four main themes (i.e., topics at the online forum) were divided into sub-themes and are summarized below with relevant quotes of the participants. Despite separate analyses, the findings on parents who partially and completely refused vaccination are described together, because they were very similar. The few differences between these two sub-groups are described at the end of the results section.

Positive and Negative Aspects of the NIP

Regarding theme one, PV and NV participants were asked to mention some positive and negative aspects of the NIP in general. Participants agreed that a positive aspect of the NIP is that it is well organized: "It is a well-organised 'machine'" (NV). Another positive is that vaccines are freely available. Participants who realized that the NIP is non-mandatory felt positive about this, too: "A positive aspect is that you have access to vaccines in The Netherlands and, as a parent, you have a free choice" (PV).

Some participants mentioned that there were too many vaccines and that vaccination in the NIP started too early: "A negative is that more and more vaccines are added" (PV). Another participant said: "I find it unfortunate that the RIVM vaccinates at a very young age when the immune system is hardly built" (NV). Another negative aspect that participants agreed upon was that they felt vaccination was mandatory, although it is not: "You get the feeling that you MUST do it. When you do not vaccinate you receive a reminder to vaccinate by post. You feel almost guilty if you do not participate" (PV).

Determinants of Vaccine Refusal

Theme two focused on parental decision-making. Various factors influenced the choice of parents to refuse vaccination partially or completely. These were related to lifestyle and parental perceptions about the body and the immune system of the child, risk perception of diseases and vaccination side effects, perceived vaccine effectiveness, the potential advantages of experiencing the disease, negative experiences with vaccination, and social environment.

Lifestyle

Lifestyle of the participants appeared an important determinant for refusing vaccination. Participants mentioned that their healthy lifestyle promotes their children's health, and therefore the risk of getting an infectious disease is reduced. Some participants focused only on nutrition: "We rely on our 'preventive' eating habits and lifestyle. Especially good nutrition ensures that you do not get ill" (NV). Other participants focused on other aspects of a healthy lifestyle, such as giving children a peaceful basis for life: "All my choices are currently aimed to give my children a peaceful basis for life: choose to breastfeed (about 1.5-2 years), raise children in a small-scale home, part-time work, first half-year no childcare, minimize shopping/travelling with young children. All kinds of things that do not overcharge the immune system" (NV).

Immune System

Most participants also mentioned that they believed that the immune system of the child was not yet adequately developed to receive vaccinations: "Administering many different viruses/bacteria at the same time seems to me a huge attack on the immune system of someone" (NV). Another participant said: "A baby's immune system has built up thanks to the mother, and it is not desirable in my eyes to give the child all kinds of substances that can disrupt the whole immune system" (PV).

Risk Perception of Disease

The risk perception of the disease is low, because some participants seemed to think that their children were not likely to contract infectious diseases and that infections were not likely to be transmitted to their child: "I also assumed, based on the fact that both children did not come that much in contact with other children at a very young age, that the risks [of getting the disease] were less" (PV). Furthermore, some participants mentioned that vaccine-preventable diseases are not that severe and can be easily treated: "Most of them [the diseases] are not life threatening and, with support of the family paediatrician or homeopathic doctor, they are easy to treat" (NV).

Risk Perception of Vaccine Side Effects

Participants who perceived little risk of the disease accordingly believed that the likelihood of negative consequences of vaccination is higher and that these consequences are more severe than getting the disease: "There are many unpleasant side effects and diseases that are due to the vaccinations, and this is always dismissed as untrue" (PV). One participant said: "We also have serious doubts about the consequences of vaccinations. [...] We also see a link between vaccinations and some behavioural problems" (NV). Other participants doubted certain components of the vaccines: "They also get many germs at once, I consider this mechanism unproven" (PV). Another participant doubted about the negative consequences of the adjuvants in vaccines: "There are adjuvants in vaccines that are poisonous, such as mercury and aluminium, and you really do not want that in your body, even in small quantities" (NV).

Perceived Efficacy of Vaccine

Participants were also worried whether or not vaccine efficacy is adequate and if vaccines would lead to protection: "Some diseases are obsolete and disease agents mutate, so the protection is not always 100%. Some vaccines work only temporarily, while the side effects may be permanent (i.e., allergies, chronic colds, autism etc.). Even though children were vaccinated, there are still epidemics (such as mumps, whooping cough)" (PV). Another participant said: "I refused vaccination against pertussis, because the effect of pertussis vaccination does not seem to be large. More and more people get pertussis, despite new vaccines and the fact that children get vaccinated at a younger age" (NV).

Perceived Advantages of Having a Disease

Some participants believed that attracting a vaccine-preventable disease was something positive for their child(ren). These participants cited the advantage of life-long immunity: "Let the body itself go through the disease. This is good for building up the resistance by the body itself. Diseases often give life-long immunity, while vaccines often protect for only 15 years" (PV). Some participants believed a child would develop physically and/or mentally after getting a disease: "You could say that the experience of a disease has a particular function; it makes a certain physical and/or mental development possible" (NV).

Negative Experience with Vaccination

A negative experience with childhood vaccination influenced the decision making of participants. Some participants were influenced by a negative story in the media: "Two years ago there was the case in which something went wrong with vaccinations for young children. Shortly after that, we refused a vaccination" (PV). Some have had a negative experience in their own environment: "Death in the family within 24 hours after vaccination…made me gain more in-depth knowledge. Together we made the choice not to vaccinate" (NV). Others cited a very personal negative experience: "Our oldest daughter (10 years) got epilepsy after vaccination. She got attacks for forty-five minutes. It was not clear to us that it was because of the vaccinations until she got such a heavy attack after the MMR vaccination that she ended up in intensive care. It's unbelievable, but doctors deny any form of adverse reactions following vaccination" (NV).

Social Environment

There were mixed findings as to whether people in the social environment influenced the parental choice to refuse vaccination. Some participants said their environment had not influenced their choice at all, whereas others said they were influenced by their friends or family members: "In my environment I had one friend who also looked critically at vaccinations. Partly because of that, I gained more in-depth knowledge" (PV). Another participant said: "I had a conversation with my mother and sister about whether to vaccinate or not. My sister did not adhere to the vaccination schedule; she vaccinated her children later than recommended" (NV). Other participants indicated that no one in their environment influenced them: "No people in our environment influenced our decision. We didn't know people who were critical towards vaccination" (NV).

Interestingly, some participants said that they did not talk about their choice to refuse vaccination with others in their environment, because they expected negative reactions: "In my environment, I sometimes have to defend why we do not follow 'the norm' [to vaccinate]" (PV). Another participant said: "We are the only ones who did not vaccinate! Our choice has often led to discussions, and more than once people showed that they thought we were crazy" (NV).

Need for Information

Theme three focused on the informational needs of participants. Many mentioned that they did not receive enough information from the RIVM about childhood vaccination: "Negative to the

NIP, I think, is that parents get absolutely no information about the vaccines. A box of paracetamol has a leaflet with a big piece of text, but about vaccinations we are only told that the puncture site may be painful, or that the child can get some fever" (PV). Participants indicated they would like to get more information about their freedom of choice: "I miss strong objective information about the background and choice options that you have as a parent, like vaccinating later…or choosing some vaccinations but not others" (PV). Specific information about the possible negative consequences of vaccines, like side effects, is also needed: "I also think that parents are not fully informed about the side effects and ingredients of vaccines by the RIVM" (PV). Another participant stated: "I would like to have open and honest information, whereby the disadvantages and risks of vaccination are discussed so parents could make a well-considered decision" (NV).

Because participants' information need was not fulfilled, they started to seek information by themselves. Some said that it was hard for them to find the right information and to make a choice to vaccinate or not, based on all the positive and negative information they found. One said: "Although I am trained to read and evaluate research, I had great difficulty to find my way in all the information" (NV). Another said: "We searched for all kinds of information, and the problem is: there is too much and you do not know how to filter. What is an opinion, what is a fact? Who is trustworthy, who is not?" (NV).

New Vaccines in the NIP

Theme four focused on possible new vaccines being added to the NIP in the future. Participants had mixed feelings whether they would accept new vaccines or not. Some said that they would refuse all new vaccines in advance, because there are already enough vaccines in the NIP: "Even more vaccinations? My goodness, I think it is already too much! Let nature take its own course, please" (PV). Other participants said they would weigh the pros and cons of each new vaccine and make a deliberate choice: "Facing new vaccines, we think the same as compared with existing vaccines: how is the vaccine tested? What is exactly in it? What would be the side effects, etcetera. We are not fundamentally against it" (PV).

Differences Between NV and PV Parents

Participants who partially or completely refused vaccination reported many similarities in the way they think and make decisions about vaccination. However, there were still some differences between the two groups. For example, participants who completely refused vaccination reported having positive experiences with not vaccinating their child(ren). They mentioned that compared to children who were vaccinated, their unvaccinated children were less often sick: "It is our experience that our child, compared with vaccinated children at his age within our environment, is less sick, and when he is sick he recovers more quickly" (NV). The participants who completely refused vaccination also discussed herd immunity, saying it was not a reason they refused vaccination. They did not depend on it to protect their unvaccinated child. Indeed, some regretted the presence of herd immunity because it reduces the chance that their child will get the disease and thereby develop natural immunity against the disease: "It is absolutely not true that our children have not been vaccinated because others do. I rather hope that my children get certain childhood illnesses at a young age than (because of the high vaccination coverage) getting the disease when they are older" (NV). These participants also mentioned that they trusted the health care in The Netherlands and believed that when their child gets sick, the quality of health care is good enough to take care of their child: "We rely on the various methods of treatment, both conventional and alternative, when we face serious diseases" (NV).

Among PV participants, we found that some had not thought beforehand about refusing a certain vaccination. Some refused or postponed vaccination simply because their child was sick at the time, and therefore was not able to receive the vaccine: "I followed my feelings and did not vaccinate my child especially when I suspected that something was troubling, like a cold or some other inconvenience" (PV). Another participant said: "The main reason [to not vaccinate] was that my daughter struggled with her health, and that I first wanted that she would be healthy before she got vaccinated" (PV).

Discussion

This study explored what factors are important in refusal of childhood vaccination by parents. Like Sporton et al., we found that most refusal of vaccination is based on deliberate decision-making of parents. Our results show that this decision is based on multiple factors, such as the lifestyle of parents, perceptions about the body and the immune system of the child, risk perception of diseases and vaccination side effects, perceived vaccine effectiveness, perceived advantages of experiencing the disease, negative experience with vaccination, and parents' social environment. In addition, this study shows that the use of online focus groups is an effective qualitative research method resulting in meaningful data.

An important determinant of refusing vaccination is the lifestyle of parents. Some of our participants stated that living a healthy life decreases the risk of getting an infectious disease. This determinant was also mentioned by Meszaros et al. This indicates that not only perceptions and beliefs about childhood vaccination are an import factor in parents' decision to refuse vaccination, but also that the general lifestyle of the parents might play a role.

Another determinant, which has also been reported by other studies is risk perception. A 2007 meta-analysis of studies linking risk perception and vaccination by Brewer et al. points to risk perception as an important factor in health behaviour. Our study shows that parents who refuse vaccination believe that the side effects of vaccines could be severe, that vaccine-preventable diseases are not that severe, and that their child is not very susceptible. These beliefs might reflect the fact that vaccine-preventable diseases have been reduced to the point that their risks seem less important than vaccination risks. It therefore seems important that public health institutes keep communicating about the severity and susceptibility of vaccine-preventable diseases.

Besides the perceived risk of disease versus vaccination, our findings as well as those of Hilton et al. suggest that parents fear the immune system in infancy is not adequately developed for a good response to vaccination. They apparently have not received enough information about the influence of vaccines on the immune system of their child, and their resulting doubts cause them to refuse vaccination.

Benin et al. showed that parents who refused vaccination reported a trusting relationship with a natural healer or some other respected person having doubts about vaccination. Our study shows similar results, in that a proportion of the parents visited an anthroposophical CWC. Besides this, some parents mentioned that experiencing a disease is positive, leading to certain physical and/or mental development. This perception seems consistent with the anthroposophical lifestyle and view about vaccination. The vaccination coverage among anthroposophists in The Netherlands is somewhat lower compared to the rest of the population, and a study of Harmsen et al. showed that parents who visited an anthroposophical CWC mostly refused the Mumps, Measles, and Rubella (MMR) vaccination because they perceive these diseases as essential for the physical and mental development of their child. These findings might indicate that parents with an anthroposophical lifestyle and/or parents who visit an anthroposophical CWC might be more critical towards childhood vaccination. However, the influence of anthroposophical CWCs on parents' decision making is so far not clear and therefore more research is needed.

Interestingly, this study showed mixed results about the influence of the social environment. As found previously, sometimes parents feel supported in vaccination refusal by their family and friends, with whom they discuss the issue. Others discuss it with no one, in part due to fear of negative responses from their community. Brown et al. mentioned that parents felt that their decision to vaccinate or not would be judged by people around them.

Mills et al. and Brown et al. showed in their studies that forgetting to make an appointment or to schedule an appointment were also factors that influenced a lower vaccination coverage. This factor was not found in this focus group study; future quantitative research is needed to explore this further.

Other studies have shown that parents need more information about childhood vaccination. Our study results showed that this is true also for Dutch parents. They would particularly like more information about the side effects of the vaccines, the components of the vaccines and more assurance that the NIP is non-mandatory.

Parents in this study indicated that when they start searching for information, it is hard to find reliable information and to make a choice from all the information they find. RIVM should therefore supply more information about childhood vaccination and also list reliable sources of additional information. In addition to official websites, social media should also be listed because of the growing proportion of online communicators, including vocal and active anti-vaccination groups. Along with the risks of non-vaccination, the official information should address the risks of vaccination. Official language should be moderate, avoiding extreme formulations, because a strong assertion that there is no risk in vaccination can paradoxically lead some people to suspect or perceive a higher risk.

Our study has both strengths and limitations. The primary strength is its use of online focus group discussions. At our online forum, parents were anonymous and therefore free to say whatever they wanted. In addition, parents could log in and respond whenever they had time, which might have resulted in a high response to every posting. Besides these strengths of the online focus group, a limitation might be that parents responded less to other parents' comments compared to face-to-face focus groups, which might have resulted in less discussion. Although qualitative studies do not seek to achieve representativeness through randomization, our study is limited by its lack of demographic information. Such information would have made findings more representative with regard to, for example, gender, educational attainment, and age. Another limitation is a possible response bias, as parents who are more negative about childhood vaccination might have been more willing to participate. Unfortunately, we have no access to information about the background of parents' non-response to our invitation. While this qualitative study provides useful insight in the factors that influence decision-making about vaccination of parents who refused vaccination, quantitative confirmation of the findings is recommended among a large population of parents to get insight in which determinants are most important.

Conclusion

This study provides an in-depth insight into the perception of parents who took the deliberate decision to refuse all or part of the free vaccinations in the Dutch NIP. Information currently provided by the RIVM turned out to be insufficient for this group of parents. They are in need of verifiable knowledge about the effects of vaccination on the development of a child's immune system; how much a healthy lifestyle can, by itself, protect children from vaccine-preventable disease; and what are the real risks, consequences and complications of such disease. At the same time, the information must increase trust in the NIP by providing more detail about vaccine side effects and more assurance that the NIP is not mandatory. Access to additional sources of reliable information should be provided. Listening to critical parents is useful for developing communication strategies that suits their concerns and reduce their feelings of ambivalence in decision making about childhood vaccinations. Further study is needed on how such information could best reach the parents who need it.

14

Why Do People Still Believe There Is a Link Between Autism and Vaccination?

Bobby Duffy

Bobby Duffy is a professor of public policy, senior research fellow, and director of the Policy Institute at King's College in London.

Incredibly, people still think vaccinations do or may cause autism, despite a lack of scientific evidence. Most of this mistrust goes back to a notorious case claiming a direct link between autism and the vaccine used to prevent MMR viruses. So many clinical and scientific studies have proven this claim to be false. Has this calmed fears? No. People have a way of hearing what they want to hear, especially when this information comes from celebrities claiming that anecdotal evidence is equal to scientific rigorous testing.

One of the most frustrating misperceptions in our many studies on what people commonly get wrong is the enduring myth that vaccines pose a risk to healthy children. It's particularly maddening because it has direct and long-lasting consequences.

Public Health England recently warned young people to look out for symptoms of measles before attending a music festival in Essex. This was in response to 12 cases being identified in the county since July, way up on usual numbers. The rise reflects a

"Autism and Vaccines: More Than Half of People in Britain, France, Italy Still Think There May Be a Link," by Bobby Duffy, The Conversation, August 22, 2018, https://theconversation.com/autism-and-vaccines-more-than-half-of-people-in-britain-france-italy-still-think-there-may-be-a-link-101930. Licensed under CC BY ND 4.0 International.

broader trend. Measles cases in Europe increased fourfold in 2017, affecting more than 20,000 people and causing 35 deaths.

In the UK, the rise in cases is often among young adults, who were less likely to be immunised as children during a period of vaccine concern sparked by Andrew Wakefield's now completely discredited claims that the MMR vaccine caused leaks in the gut that went through the bloodstream to the brain.

But new doubts keep being layered on, with points about freedom of choice from Italian political parties muddying the waters, and more than 20 tweets from the US president, Donald Trump, suggesting a link. This is despite many reviews that fail to find any link, including a 2014 meta-analysis of records from over 1.25m children.

Have these unfounded fears stuck with the public around the world? Our first ever multi-country study, in 38 nations, on vaccine misperceptions suggests they have. Around one in every five people believe that "some vaccines cause autism in healthy children," and 38% are unsure whether it is true or not.

The proportions positively believing it is true ranged from an incredible 44% in India, down to 8% in Spain.

But there are majorities in many countries who think it's true or are unsure: in France it's 65%, in Britain it's 55%, in Italy it's 52%. And even in countries where it's not quite a majority who think it's true or are unsure, it's often only just below: in Sweden it's 49% and in the US and Germany it's 48%.

Why Do We Fear Vaccines?

So why do three in five people across these countries feel unsure or believe that there actually is a link between some vaccines and autism in healthy children, despite the claims being so widely discredited? It is partly because it has many of the ingredients that drive conspiracy theories.

First, it's a highly emotive issue—there is little more emotional than the health of our children. We treat information differently when we are in highly emotional states, being more sensitised and less considered or rational.

Second, it involves medical complexity and requires an understanding of risk, which we really struggle with. In particular, we need to understand the distinction between hazard, which is the potential for harm, and risk, which is the probability of that adverse outcome actually happening. For example, there is an incredibly small but real chance that a vaccine could aggravate an underlying mitochondrial disorder, which has been linked to regressive autism in a miniscule fraction of children. There are US court rulings that we could legitimately take as evidence of this being a hazard, but they are vanishingly rare, and the risk is therefore effectively non-existent. But that is a difficult point to communicate.

In addition, the communications we do see on vaccines are often actively unhelpful, with sections of the media keeping these stories alive. This does not just mean television shows or articles that give space to those who make the case for the vaccine–autism link without providing space for counter claims.

Then there is also a more subtle effect from "balanced" reporting. This is where a media item says that while a credible source disagrees with a position, some others still believe it. There is increasing evidence that this apparent balance actually serves to polarise, because we have directionally motivated reasoning, where we pick what we want from the evidence. Cass Sunstein, in studies on reactions to contradictory information on climate change, has called this "asymmetrical updating," where people take the information that fits with their views, and ignore the counter evidence.

The narrative across all these sources is also important. Stories stick with us, and there are a lot of individual case study claims in the vaccine–autism link. Jenny McCarthy, the model, actress and television presenter, is the highest profile "autism mom" and regularly explains how she's told by "thousands" of other parents how, following vaccination, "I came home, he had a fever, he stopped speaking, and then he became autistic." Elevating these stories to be on a par with representative evidence, McCarthy says, without a hint of irony that "parents' anecdotal information is science-based information."

In these environments, the story takes over from reality. Paul Offit, a vaccine scientist, refuses to appear with McCarthy in media interviews, as he explains: "Every story has a hero, victim, and villain. McCarthy is the hero, her child is the victim—and that leaves one role for you."

The contrast with early days of vaccines couldn't be greater. When Jonas Salk announced the results of his polio vaccine tests there were 16 television cameras filming the dry, academic presentation, relaying the outcome to 54,000 physicians across the country—judges even suspended trials so people could celebrate the results. It was as if a war had ended, said one observer.

In some ways, vaccines are a victim of their own success, because we are much more likely to notice phantom scares than world-changing but incremental improvements. We need to fight these frighteningly widespread vaccine misperceptions to avoid a much more attention-grabbing reverse.

15

The Spread of Fake Science Is Impacted by Online Searches

Nadia Arif, et al.

Nadia Arif, Manuela Mengozzi, and Pietro Ghezzi are affiliated with Brighton and Sussex Medical School. Majed Al-Jefri is affiliated with the School of Computing, Engineering and Mathematics at the University of Brighton. Isabella Harb Bizzi is affiliated with Universidade Federal do Rio Grande do Sul. Gianni Boitano Perano and Inam Haq are affiliated with Sydney Medical School. Michel Goldman and Marie Neunez are affiliated with the Institute for Interdisciplinary Innovation in Healthcare, Universite libre de Bruxelles. Kee Leng Chua and Helen Smith are affiliated with Lee Kong Chian School of Medicine, Nanyang Technological University.

The following excerpted viewpoint is a study analyzing online information available to the public on the link between vaccines and autism around the globe. The premise is that the Lancet *paper connecting the MMR vaccine with autism still carries a great deal of weight, even though that paper has been discredited. It is interesting to see how articles were ranked in Google searches, thus influencing the public on something as important as their health.*

"Fake News or Weak Science? Visibility and Characterization of Antivaccine Webpages Returned by Google in Different Languages and Countries," by Nadia Arif, Majed Al-Jefri, Isabella Harb Bizzi, Gianni Boitano Perano, Michel Goldman, Inam Haq, Kee Leng Chua, Manuela Mengozzi, Marie Neunez, Helen Smith and Pietro Ghezzi, Frontiers Media S.A., June 5, 2018. https://www.frontiersin.org/articles/10.3389/fimmu.2018.01215/full#h5. Licenced under CC BY 4.0 International.

The 1998 *Lancet* paper by Wakefield et al., despite subsequent retraction and evidence indicating no causal link between vaccinations and autism, triggered significant parental concern. The aim of this study was to analyze the online information available on this topic. Using localized versions of Google, we searched "autism vaccine" in English, French, Italian, Portuguese, Mandarin, and Arabic and analyzed 200 websites for each search engine result page (SERP). A common feature was the newsworthiness of the topic, with news outlets representing 25–50% of the SERP, followed by unaffiliated websites (blogs, social media) that represented 27–41% and included most of the vaccine-negative websites. Between 12 and 24% of websites had a negative stance on vaccines, while most websites were pro-vaccine (43–70%). However, their ranking by Google varied. While in Google.com, the first vaccine-negative website was the 43rd in the SERP, there was one vaccine-negative webpage in the top 10 websites in both the British and Australian localized versions and in French and two in Italian, Portuguese, and Mandarin, suggesting that the information quality algorithm used by Google may work better in English. Many webpages mentioned celebrities in the context of the link between vaccines and autism, with Donald Trump most frequently. Few websites (1–5%) promoted complementary and alternative medicine (CAM) but 50–100% of these were also vaccine-negative suggesting that CAM users are more exposed to vaccine-negative information. This analysis highlights the need for monitoring the web for information impacting on vaccine uptake.

Introduction

Acceptance and uptake of vaccination is important for reaching public health targets. The information available, either from books, television news, newspaper articles, or online sources, has a major impact on how the public perceives vaccines. In this respect, the most impactful information was the publication by Andrew Wakefield in the medical journal the *Lancet* in 1998, supporting a link between the mumps, measles, and rubella (MMR) vaccine and autism. The journal eventually retracted the paper in 2010, because its findings were discredited, but its message has become commonplace and remains a significant concern among parents.

It has often been pointed out that antivaccine information available on the Internet has a high prevalence and could impact negatively vaccination decisions. Observational studies have shown an association between exposure to antivaccine information on Twitter, and on the Internet in general, and a negative perception of vaccine risks. A Canadian study on 250 mothers also reported that reliance on governmental websites, which promote vaccination, is associated with higher vaccination rates. It is difficult, however, to draw a causal link from these associations and quantify the impact of online information on vaccine uptake.

Furthermore, the information on the prevalence of antivaccine websites is not consistent. A study in the USA analyzing 89 websites on human papilloma virus (HPV) returned by Google, Yahoo, and Bing reported less than 10% of websites with negative tone about vaccines while one on MMR, also in the USA, reported that searching Google in 2014 returned a proportion of 41% of antivaccine websites.

The purpose of this study is to analyze the information available to the public, 20 years on from the publication of the above mentioned *Lancet* paper, on the link between vaccines and autism. The study does not analyze the impact of online information of vaccination rates or on public health views on vaccines but provides an approach to monitor vaccine-related information on the web. Using a methodology used previously for similar studies, we obtained a sample of the existing information using Google as the search engine. This captures most information as news outlets, television, books, professional or government organizations, scientific journals, and personal websites or blogs are all online. We sampled the first 200 results returned by Google searching for "autism vaccines," and analyzed them for the vaccines mentioned, their stance on vaccination, and the source of the website. We also used a standard indicator of health information quality, the

JAMA score, to assess their basic trustworthiness index. The JAMA score considers whether a website declares author, date of writing, financial ownership, and whether its information is backed up by references.

The analysis was performed in different countries on localized versions of the search engine in different languages (google.com, google.co.uk, and google.com.au in English; google.be in French; google.it in Italian; google.com.br in Portuguese; google.com.sg in Mandarin; google.com.sa in Arabic). This research was done by a pre-existing international research collaboration, and that dictated the choice of the languages or localized versions of Google.

We also investigated the visibility, in terms of ranking, given by the search engine to webpages with a negative tone on vaccines. This has been overlooked by most studies, and it is known that users typically spend a short time on each website and seldom go beyond the first ones in the search engine result page (SERP).

The results indicate differences in the composition of the antivaccine websites across the world and the footprint left by Wakefield's *Lancet* paper. They also show differences in the ranking of antivaccine websites in the different localized versions of Google.

Materials and Methods

We searched the two keywords "vaccines" and "autism" in Google between June and September 2017. It was decided to use only those keywords because we wanted to obtain a sample of the websites returned independently of the expression used. For this reason, we decided not to use questions such as "do vaccines cause autism?" because the results would be different depending on how the question was formulated and we needed to be consistent across the different languages. Although "vaccines" could be synonymous to "immunization," particularly in the scientific literature, we decided to use the search term "vaccines" as this best represents what the lay public would search on the Internet.

Before performing the search, the investigators deleted cookies and browsing history from their browsers to avoid the results of the search being influenced by previous searches done on the same computer, although it must be noted that the search engine will still identify the locations where the searches was made from the IP address, and this may customize results. Locations where the searches were performed were as follows: google.com (English), google.co.uk (English), google.it (Italian), and google.com.sa (Arabic), Brighton, UK; google.com.au (English), Sydney, NSW, Australia; google.be (French), Brussels, Belgium; google.com.sg (Mandarin), Singapore; google.com.br (Portuguese), Porto Alegre, Brazil.

The first 200 websites returned in each SERP were transferred to a spreadsheet and then the websites visited individually. When searching google.be, the French terms (vaccins, autisme) were used and any webpage in Flemish would be excluded from the analysis. Webpages that were deemed not relevant, for instance, not mentioning vaccines or aggregators, like those no longer accessible, behind a paywall or requiring registration were excluded from the analysis.

The total number of webpages considered for the analysis were as follows: English (Google.com), 175; English, UK, 188; English, Australia,194; French, 154; Portuguese, 132; Italian, 191; Mandarin, 179; Arabic, 146.

For each website, we recorded the typology of the website using the classification previously described. The typologies considered were: Commercial (C), Government (G), Health portal (HP), News (N), No-profit (NP), Professional (P), scientific journals (SJ). Those not fitting any of these categories or difficult to classify are listed as "others" (O). These included blogs, personal websites, or websites not affiliated with any of the other typologies.

To assess the JAMA score, we searched the webpage for the presence of the following information: author, date, references, owner of website.

We also annotated webpages according to the following features: (1) The name of the vaccine mentioned; (2) the overall stance on vaccines (positive, negative, or neutral); (3) the chemicals or adjuvants mentioned; (4) whether the page mentioned complementary and alternative medicine (CAM) and its stance toward it (positive, neutral, or negative); (5) whether religion was mentioned; (6) whether the page contained a testimonial (e.g., a personal story); (7) whether a celebrity was mentioned. For websites associated with the typology "News," we recorded the most mentioned stories in each SERP.

[…]

Discussion

The varied composition of the SERP returned by Google, with only 30% being non-affiliated websites or blogs, and the rest representing a wide range of news outlets, professional or government organizations, and scientific journals, represents a good sample of the information on the topic of vaccines and autism that the public is exposed to.

Because we analyzed the first 200 websites returned by Google, the list is not just a sample of all that is available in what has been called the infosphere, but it also reflects the visibility, or ranking, given by Google. For this reason, we did not just look at the composition of the SERP but also how webpages are ranked, particularly, the first 10 results that are more likely to be read.

Despite retraction of his paper in 2010, Dr. Wakefield is still highly mentioned (a word count found his name recurring 462 times in the Google.com search, 551 in UK, 706 in Australia, 378 in French, 361 in Italian, 21 in Arabic, 195 in Portuguese, and 11 in Mandarin). Although his original paper did not appear in any SERP, a letter he published in the *Lancet* in 1999 was present in both the UK and the Australian SERP (but not Google.com). In French, two websites (one Belgian and one French) displayed a video of Andrew Wakefield's interview with subtitles in French.

It is important to be aware that the autism-MMR scare was not borne out of an obscure sect but from scientific papers published in respectable and authoritative journals, leading to a widespread concern even among health professionals.

This seems to be true today when articles published in academic journals of varied respectability can have a significant impact as they may be perceived as providing a scientific basis for antivaccine, or just vaccine-skeptical, positions. A study has shown that, in the US, a drop in the MMR vaccination rate was observed soon after the publication of original scientific reports, even before this was the subject of media coverage. These may also be ranked higher by search engines because scientific articles may be considered authoritative and, therefore, proxies for high quality information.

It may be surprising that in the UK and Australian websites, but not in Google.com, a proportion of SJs were vaccine-negative. As mentioned above, very few websites of SJs were present in non-English SERPs, not surprisingly as scientific articles are usually in English. Of the six scientific articles in Google.com, none were vaccine-negative, whereas UK and Australian websites (13 scientific articles each) had some vaccine-negative scientific articles (three and one, respectively). In the UK SERP, three vaccine-negative scientific papers were found. One was a 2002 paper in *LabMedicine*, published by the Oxford University Press and the American Society for Clinical Pathology and, to our knowledge, never retracted; a second a letter by Wakefield published in the *Lancet* in 1999 in response to criticism over his previous paper; a third is a 2017 editorial published in the "Madridge Journal of Vaccines," a journal published in the US but, unlike the *Lancet* and *LabMedicine*, not listed by PubMed and the National Library of Medicine.

In particular, the 2002 paper published by Oxford University Press was ranked second in the UK SERP. Repeating the "autism vaccines" search on Google.co.uk 6 months later still returned this article second in the ranking. This online article was not found in Google.com or in the Australian SERP.

In the Australian search, two websites were collections of scientific papers supporting a causal link between vaccines and autism, a third the Wakefield letter mentioned above, and a fourth a paper by the organization "Informed Consent Action Network" that, even if not published in a journal, and it might be questionable whether it could be legitimately defined a scientific paper as it is unclear whether it was peer reviewed, has all the features of a scientific review. Classifying these papers as vaccine-negative was a shared but subjective decision of the authors who reviewed those websites, and we provide the references in case the reader wishes to reassess our coding from a different perspective.

As noted in a *Nature* editorial by Leask, "just four months after the publication that triggered the MMR scare, 13% of general practitioners and 27% of practice nurses in north Wales thought it very likely or possible that the vaccine was associated with autism." Leask noted that, to improve uptake of vaccinations, we should engage "fence-sitting parents." This means that pro-immunization information needs to address those issues and concerns that anti-vaccine websites raise, such as the mention of aluminum or mercury as a component of thimerosal, as highlighted by our study. Furthermore, the present study also advocates the dissemination of pro-vaccine information on the same websites typologies that perpetuate the "fake science" that vaccines cause autism.

Despite the science behind it being discredited, there are several reasons as to why the association between the MMR vaccine and autism is still present amongst the lay public. Flaherty pointed out that this is partly due to autism being a complex condition without a single, established causal mechanism. It should be noted that a search of websites mentioning "vaccines and autism" returns websites mentioning other vaccines, not just the MMR, as this could suggest a potential extrapolation of the link with autism to other types of vaccines.

The strong association between vaccine-negative stance and CAM, as well as commercial websites often selling "natural products," confirms that cultural factors may reinforce an antivaccine stance by the association of vaccines with capitalism, big pharma, and profit.

Another finding of the present study is that government organizations accounted for only 1.3–6.7% of websites. This is markedly less than what we found previously in a study on influenza vaccine where governmental websites represented 17% of the SERP in English and 42% of that in Italian. The reason for this is probably that, in the present study, we specifically introduced the search term "autism," which may not be mentioned in most of the government websites unless for educational purpose, which is to explain that there is no link to autism. The other possibility is that, in the case of influenza, there is a strong vaccination campaign because it is done on a voluntary basis, while the MMR is either part of the routine immunization schedule of babies (e.g., UK) or compulsory (e.g., Italy since 2017 or France for babies born after 01/01/2018).

The fact that Trump is the most frequently mentioned celebrity reminds us of the difference between countries, where in some countries antivaccine sentiment is prevalent among alternative, left-wing groups, and right-wing, individualist, groups in others. We could not find a significant association between mention of religious issues and sentiment about vaccines. In fact, religious beliefs may be important in the confidence in vaccines, although this may be a confounder as there are few religious groups who officially reject vaccinations.

The fact that news outlets represent 30–50% of the websites indicates that the link between vaccine and autism is a topical and newsworthy topic. From this point of view, it is reassuring that news websites returned by Google have a low frequency of vaccine-negative articles. This is not to say that there are no antivaccine news articles (many vaccine-negative articles have been published by top tabloid newspapers in the UK) but rather that these are not given visibility by the algorithm used by Google.

However, the information quality criteria used by Google do not always penalize vaccine-negative websites. This study shows that, while in Google.com the first vaccine-negative webpage came up only as 43rd, in the local UK and Australian SERPs some were found in the first 10 websites, and this was even more marked in non-English SERPs.

Interestingly, this is similar to what we observed in a previous research where we analyzed the information returned by Google on influenza vaccine or influenza prevention in English and Italian. While in Google.com in English there were no vaccine-negative websites or websites promoting non-evidence-based medicine approaches to influenza prevention, this was not true for a search in Italian.

Of course, here we only use Google as a mesh to collect a sample of the web and the websites returned in the SERP might just reflect "what is out there." However, it is important to note that the overall frequency of vaccine-negative webpages was not so different in the different SERPs, and we have no explanation for this observation. One wonders whether the vaccine-negative study published in a SJ was ranked high in the UK SERP because the publisher is Oxford University Press, or whether the one in the top 10 in the Australian SERP was ranked high because the .org domain was taken as a proxy of authority and quality. It is also possible that the higher ranking of vaccine-negative webpages in some SERPs is due to the fact that they receive a high number of clicks in that country or language.

Another interesting finding of this study is the difference in the JAMA score of different SERPs. Websites in Arabic showed the lowest JAMA score than all other languages. Websites from Google.com and Google.co.uk ranked higher than those from the localized versions in English-Australia, French, and Italian. The fact that the mean JAMA score of websites returned in the Australian SERP is also significantly lower than that of those returned by Google.com or Google.UK seem to exclude that the language alone explains the difference.

One obvious question is how much the antivaccine information impacts on the uptake of vaccines. Data from the Organization for Economic Co-operation and Development (OECD) show that, in 2015, Italy had the lowest vaccination rate for measles (85%), People's Republic of China the highest (99%), Australia and France 91%, the USA 92%, the UK 95%, Belgium and Brazil 96%, Portugal and Saudi Arabia, 98%. The low immunization rate is the reason why the Italian government made the MMR vaccine compulsory in July 2017, France followed in 2018 and Australia is also going along that route.

We assessed whether there was a correlation between the percentage of vaccine-negative webpages and either the safety-related skepticism in the countries analyzed or with the uptake of measles vaccination in 2016 (data from https://data.worldbank.org/indicator/SH.IMM.MEAS). There was no statistically significant correlation using the Spearman-Rank test or the Pearson correlation coefficient.

It should also be noted that the search in Mandarin was performed using the localized version of Google in Singapore; because the Google search engine is not available in the People's Republic of China, our results cannot be extrapolated to the information available in that country. We should also bear in mind that most of the languages investigated are not specific to a single country. Hence, making correlation between webpages in one language and vaccination rate or sentiment in one country, is not immediate.

This lack of correlation might support the view that the impact of online information on vaccination acceptance may be exaggerated. For instance, a study among French mothers reported that the main source of information on vaccination is the family physician or pediatrician (84–90%) and the Internet accounts for only 10–12%, while a study on 1737 Canadian parents showed that, to obtain trustworthy and reliable information on vaccines, 68% of them would ask a physician, and just 27% the Internet. If we also consider the fact that only a small percentage of parents refuse to vaccinate their children, one could conclude that we should not overestimate the impact of webpages with a vaccine-negative stance. Other issues may be at the basis of vaccine skepticism such as the perceived role of big pharma and governments or the underestimation of potential risks, as in the case of the dengue vaccine.

A major limitation of this study is that we only looked at webpages and did not investigate social networks. Studies have previously explored this area of the Internet and have analyzed their features in English and French. Another limitation of the present study is that we analyzed the sample of the online information on the topic but not all websites will have the same impact. Even within the first ten results, readers may just briefly glance through them using clues to decide what to read. To assess which top-ranking websites attract attention of the user and are actually read, research should be undertaken by asking volunteers to rank websites or, alternatively, their attention could be monitored using eye-tracking software. A further limitation of our study is that we used the same, neutral, search string ("vaccine autism") without taking into account potential differences in the most searched terms used, which could well be different in different languages. It is likely that users could find more biased information by using more negative search terms, although a recent study using eye-tracking software to investigate the search behavior of 56 volunteers found that users are more likely to use neutral search terms.

In summary, the main findings of this study are the marked differences in the visibility of websites with a negative stance on vaccines given by the ranking by Google across not only different languages but also in different localized searches in English. Public health authorities, particularly those acting internationally, will need to take these differences into account when designing websites aiming at promoting vaccinations. They will also need to consider the relevance that issues like the adjuvants included in vaccine preparation have in the information available and clarify these issues to correct misinformation. Counteracting disinformation about vaccines by health authorities is part of the solution, but the loss of confidence in vaccines goes far beyond misinformation. Communities, social environment, educational level, are a few examples of factors affecting the vaccine confidence. Education, as well as transparency, would be an important aspect to keep in mind when trying to increase vaccine confidence.

16

Be a Smart Tourist Because Disease Can Spread Through Travel

World Travel & Tourism Council

The World Travel & Tourism Council is an organization that works to raise awareness about the tourism industry. The council's priorities are security and travel facilitation, crisis preparedness, management and recovery, and sustainable growth.

The World Travel & Tourism Council examines a couple of points about travel in the following viewpoint. With the speed of travel and the ease of flying between continents, the chance of being exposed to disease or carrying a disease to another location is possible. The council gives timely reminders about how to travel smart when health epidemics are occurring. It also emphasizes that the local recipients of the traveling public depend upon the tourism to continue for their economies.

Twelve years ago, I was flying to Shanghai with my mother and sister. We were in economy class, but each of us had a whole row of seats to sleep on for the long-distance flight. Immigration and baggage collection was similarly convenient and smooth. Except for an additional fever screening perhaps—it was the height of the SARS epidemic, which was spreading from China around the region and would come to infect over 8,000 people.

"Tourism and the Spread of Disease," World Travel & Tourism Council, Medium, August 19, 2015. Reprinted by permission.

With shorter queues and lower prices, it was arguably a great time to travel to China. And, for the Travel and Tourism sector, it was vital that people continued doing so. When health epidemics scare people off travelling, the impact is felt immediately by airlines, hotels, tour operators, and all the other businesses that depend on travellers' money.

At the same time, it's clear that all the global travel that is such an integral part of our economic and social reality today is also one of the main risk factors in the spread of viruses and diseases around the world. Along with the growth in aviation, the world is getting more and more connected. A study by a team from MIT found that the links between regions created by the global aviation network increased by 140% between 1990 and 2012.

Over 3.3 billion people took a flight in 2014, and with just a connection or two each one of these could get to pretty much anywhere in the world to anywhere else. Adding the fact that air passengers travel in close proximity in the sealed environment of a plane, it is easy to see why aviation is seen as a major risk factor in the spread of a global epidemic.

Leaving melodramatic Hollywood representations such as 2011's *Contagion* aside, real examples have shown that it doesn't take many people to spread an epidemic around the world. The global SARS outbreak in 2003 was catalysed by just ten international visitors who were staying at the same hotel as a SARS-ill Chinese physician. These ten guests travelled on to destinations throughout the world before knowing they were carrying the virus with them and igniting chains of transmissions around the world.

So how can modern travellers strike the right balance in not unnecessarily increasing the danger of epidemics while at the same time avoiding drastic disruptions to Travel and Tourism, to say nothing of their own businesses and lives?

Of course, there are certain basics that should be quite obvious. Travelling to the direct site of an acute outbreak is never good practice, without a good reason to do so. And in all cases, travellers should always clearly follow health authorities' instructions and restrictions, even if they may pose an inconvenience or disruption to original plans. Spending a week or two in quarantine may not be fun, but there are certain sacrifices we need to make in the interest of global health (if not just even for your own safety). More fundamentally, basic personal care practices—hand washing, limiting contact with visibly ill people, awareness of any potential symptoms—are best pursued with special vigilance when travelling.

Adherence to official guidance, general hygiene, and (what should be) common sense aside, the existence of a health concern is not always an automatic reason to abandon travel. In most cases, the true risk is nowhere close to how it is perceived.

Sometimes, the biggest impact from a health epidemic comes from completely misguided responses to a situation. A poignant example comes from travellers who cancelled their trips to South Africa at the time of the Ebola outbreak in East Africa. This despite the fact that Cape Town is farther away from Sierra Leone than London is and not much closer than New York.

In places where tourists do not pose an added risk to the spread of a disease, and in which they are not in danger of catching it themselves, a reduction in tourism flows and the corresponding loss of revenue only adds further damage to destinations already burdened by the health situation.

A recent demonstration of the dramatic impact a health situation can have on tourism is the case of South Korea following the MERS outbreak. Within just two weeks of the first case of the virus in the country, over 20,000 foreign travellers cancelled their planned trips. And according to travel intelligence company ForwardKeys, net bookings for trips to South Korea decreased by over 99% in the month following the first case of MERS in the country. A sudden, and unpredictable drop, in tourist arrivals such as this can have debilitating impact on the Travel and Tourism sector and beyond, especially in a country like South Korea, where tourism has been playing an important role in a struggling economy.

An absence of tourist visitors impacts the entire system of the far-reaching tourism sector. No guests means no income for the hotels, restaurants, destinations, shops, and everyone else who caters to them. And since epidemics usually hit quite rapidly and unexpectedly, tourism businesses do not have a chance to adapt to a changing number of tourists. As a result, airlines may have to fly almost empty planes, hotel employees have no guests to serve, and an entire tourism season can quickly be derailed.

Again, there are certainly situations when this loss is a necessary and unavoidable cost to address more pressing health risks. But in others, as much normality as possible—in tourism as well as other areas—is often the best prescription to limit the negative impact of an epidemic.

Ultimately, each person has to make the decision they are comfortable with in the end. And perhaps that judgment is somewhat different for a family travelling with young children from what it is for a businesswoman with an important contract to sign.

But, in any case, just because the media has mentioned a disease outbreak isn't necessarily a reason to cancel your trip. And, in fact, you might even get to enjoy a bit more legroom instead!

17

The Flu Shot Does a Good Job, but It Is Not Fail-Safe

Maggie Fox

Maggie Fox is a writer, editor, and journalist covering science and medicine. Fox has worked with many news outlets, most recently as senior writer with NBC News.

There are always people who say that they've gotten the flu after getting the flu vaccine. Is is true? The medical community admits this to be a possibility but also suggests that people might be getting sick with another type of virus and blaming the symptoms on the flu shot. In any case, the flu vaccine that comes out every year is the best way to prevent cases of the flu or lessen the severity of the disease if caught while vaccinated.

V accines have wiped out smallpox and they've nearly eradicated polio. Vaccination can control measles and mumps, and they protect travelers against yellow fever and cholera.

Most are so good that a few doses in childhood cover people for decades, even life. But there's one vaccine that people have to get every single year, and even then it's not guaranteed to fully prevent infection. It's the flu shot, and scientists are struggling to find a way to make a better one.

Debbie Fauver believes in flu vaccines—so much so that she brings home a batch of syringes to immunize her family every

"Flu Shot Fail: Why Doesn't the Vaccine Always Work?" by Maggie Fox, NBC Universal, February 9, 2014. Reprinted by permission.

year. She's a nurse, working at a hospital in Greenville, Ky., and vaccinated her grown children and husband last November. She was surprised when her 25-year-old daughter Molly got the flu anyway.

"It hit her quick," Fauver told NBC News. Molly developed back pain, chill and a fever of 101 degrees. Knowing prompt treatment can make a difference, Fauver advised her daughter to visit a doctor right away, where an on-the-spot test confirmed she had influenza and she was treated with a pill called Tamiflu.

"The doctors seem to think that her flu strain probably wasn't covered in the flu shot," Fauver says.

That's one possibility. Flu mutates like crazy and there are dozens of different strains, and hundreds of possibilities. In any one season three to four strains could be circulating and making people sick, which is why this year's vaccines protect against three or four strains—H1N1, H3N2 and either one or two B strains.

"There's a little bit of a guessing game each year. Sometimes it's not a good match," says Dr. Alicia Fry, a physician with the Centers for Disease Control and Prevention's Influenza Division. But even when the vaccine is a close match—when the virus strains that are infecting more people are the same strains used to make the vaccine—some people get sick even when they have been vaccinated.

The CDC usually reports in mid-February on how well that season's vaccine is performing. This year so far, virtually everyone who has had influenza, had it tested and had it typed, has had H1N1 flu—a strain that's included in the vaccines. It's been about an average flu season, and flu seems to be on the wane, but 40 children have been reported killed by the virus so far this year.

In 2012, the CDC says, the flu vaccine kept 80,000 people out of the hospital, even though just 45 percent of Americans who should have been vaccinated did so. At a 70 percent vaccination rate, 110,000 more people would have been spared a hospital visit, the CDC estimates.

In any given year, on average, flu vaccines are about 60 percent effective—although they're more effective than that in children. "We are trying to understand this. We are trying to make vaccines better," says Fry.

One worrying finding that has popped up on occasion seems to suggest that people who get vaccinated every year, as recommended, may sometimes have less protection than people who don't get regularly vaccinated.

Most recent was a study done last year by Dr. Arnold Monto and colleagues at the University of Michigan, who found that people vaccinated two years in a row didn't seem protected against flu at all. But it was a very small group of people and it would be important to do a larger study designed specifically to ask that question, Monto says. Of the 125 people who tested positive for flu, 59 percent had been vaccinated, his team found.

"We think that this is a good vaccine. It's not a great vaccine," Monto said. "We think that the disease that you get if you get vaccinated and still get infected is a milder disease. We are trying to document that."

Fry notes that people who choose to be vaccinated every year may be different from people who don't for many reasons "They tend to be older," she said. They often have other conditions, such as diabetes, high blood pressure or asthma.

"We are trying very hard to understand prior vaccination and what it really means, but I think at this point we don't understand it and we can't explain it in a simple way," Fry added.

"The bottom line is that, at this point, vaccination is the best prevention strategy that we have."

One reason that it's hard to study the issue of prior vaccination is that it's not considered ethical to do a randomized study—one in which people are randomly assigned to either get a vaccine or not and then watched to see if they get sick, says Dr. John Treanor of the University of Rochester in New York, who helps develop and test flu vaccines.

So studies have to be done in the very complicated, messy real world. People who routinely get vaccinated may be different from people who don't. They may be more likely to report—or admit—they are ill, for instance.

And other studies have shown just the opposite—that people who get vaccinated more often have better protection. That's been shown more clearly in kids than adults. "I think the jury is still out," Treanor said.

And there is always the issue of influenza itself, changing and mutating a lot some years, and not at all in others. From the mid-1970s to 2009, more than 30 years, the H3N2 strain dominated. Then in 2009 the pandemic H1N1 swine flu, a very distant relative of the "Spanish flu" that wiped out millions in 1918, came into the mix.

Last year, H1N1 didn't do much at all. And now this year, it's the dominant strain again. This unpredictable pattern would make it hard to advise people to do anything but just get vaccinated, Treanor says.

"It's conceivable that if you were vaccinated last year and there was no change in the vaccine composition from the year before, that you wouldn't need to be vaccinated," Treanor said. "But as a public health policy, it would be very hard to implement."

Scientists at government agencies, universities and drug companies are all trying to solve this problem by working towards a so-called universal flu vaccine. That's one that would protect against all, or most, flu strains.

They've improved vaccines a little bit and this season scientists are watching closely to see if the changes have an effect. For instance, there's a new high-dose vaccine formulated to protect seniors better. Older people who have weakened immune systems don't mount much of a defense to disease when they are vaccinated.

There are so-called quadrivalent fomulations, which protect against four different strains of flu instead of three.

No flu vaccine protects people as well as a natural infection with influenza, Monto notes. But no one suggests skipping the vaccine and going for that natural infection—flu puts hundreds of thousands of people into the hospital every year, and kills anywhere between 3,000 and 49,000 people, including many young, perfectly healthy people.

"We all admit these are not optimal vaccines. They are the best we have," Fry said.

The admission may provide convenient excuses to people who don't want to get vaccinated. But the CDC notes that 75 percent of the illnesses people get after they're vaccinated are not flu, but are caused by other viruses such as rhinoviruses, coronaviruses, parainfluenza viruses and dozens more.

And even Fauver isn't put off by her daughter's experience. "I would still take one every year and I recommend flu shots to everybody," she said.

18

The Future Promises Better Flu Vaccines

Marla Broadfoot

Marla Broadfoot is a freelance science writer and editor working out of North Carolina. She has a Ph.D. in genetics and is a contributing editor to American Scientist Magazine.

For anyone interested in avoiding the flu, the vaccination against it has been acceptable at best. Even during a good year, many people still end up getting the virus. Scientists and researchers now think they know why and are doing something about it. Researchers hope that their new techniques in vaccine production will soon make the shot better at preventing disease.

For decades, vaccine manufacturers have used chicken eggs to grow the flu virus strains included in the seasonal flu shot. But because these human strains frequently mutate to adapt to their new environment in eggs, the resulting vaccine is often an imperfect match to the actual virus that it is supposed to protect against.

Duke researchers have devised a way to keep the human influenza virus from mutating during production, generating a perfect match to the target vaccine in a shorter time frame. Their findings appear in the journal *mBio*.

"We have solved a fundamental problem that scientists had accepted would be part of vaccine production—that the virus is always going to mutate if it is grown in eggs," said senior study author Nicholas S. Heaton, Ph.D., assistant professor of molecular genetics and microbiology at Duke University School of Medicine. "This research could lead to a significantly cheaper and more efficacious vaccine."

The influenza vaccine has been notoriously ineffective. During the 2015–2016 flu season, the vaccine reduced the risk of catching a serious bout of the flu by just 42 percent, and that was considered a good year. Most of the time, the vaccine's lackluster performance is blamed on poor strain selection. The World Health Organization tracks which virus strains are circulating and decides which ones should go into the vaccine each year. Because they have to pick months in advance, and the virus is constantly evolving, they sometimes miss the mark.

Yet sometimes they pick the right strain, and still people who get the vaccine aren't adequately protected. A few years ago, scientists figured out why: the receptor that the virus uses to get into cells is shaped differently in a human nose than it is in a chicken egg. The human virus has to alter the key it carries with it—a protein called hemagglutinin (HA)—so that it can operate in its new locale. Because hemagglutinin also happens to be the part of the flu vaccine that induces an immune response in people (it's the H in a virus name like H5N1), each mutation renders the vaccine less effective.

Heaton and his team attempted to engineer a virus that would both grow happily in chicken eggs and produce the HA protein required to protect people. They expressed two versions of hemagglutinin—one adapted to eggs and one adapted to humans—on one virus particle.

"We reasoned that the egg-adapted HA would do all the heavy lifting," Heaton said. "It could do the virus entry work and just bring the other (human) one along for the ride. In effect, that would alleviate the strong selective pressure on the human HA to mutate."

Heaton and his colleagues constructed this "bivalent," or two-strain, virus and grew it in chicken cells. They showed that it packaged twice as much protein as a "monovalent" virus that carries just one HA. When they vaccinated mice with either the bivalent or monovalent vaccine (both with genetically identical human HA proteins), they found equal immune responses across the board.

Next, the researchers wanted to see if their technology could tackle some of the worst-growing vaccine strains in history. In 2002, the Fujian strain grew so poorly in production that, although it was the major circulating strain that the time, it could not be included in the vaccine. As a result, nobody was vaccinated against Fujian that year, and vaccine efficacy was very poor.

Heaton and his team plugged the HA from that infamous Fujian strain into their egg-adapted system and rescued the virus right off the bat. When the two HA proteins were put together, it grew five orders of magnitude more virus.

After the researchers had grown the virus in chicken eggs for a while, they harvested the virus and sequenced the human HA protein. They did not find a single mutation.

"Because viruses typically mutate during vaccine production, manufacturers have to screen for mutations, and decide which ones can be tolerated and which ones can't," Heaton said. "If we can eliminate mutations, we can cut back dramatically on production time."

Though the technology is still in its infancy, the researchers have successfully used it to make bivalent viruses with a half dozen different HA molecules. Currently, they are making their own versions of the vaccines that are under production for the 2017 and 2018 flu seasons, and are planning to test how they differ in terms of growth, genetic stability, and actual protection.

"There's a laundry list of problems with the flu vaccine, but this is something that we can solve now, not 10 or 15 years down the line," said Heaton. "We're not proposing to change any kind of vaccine production or vaccine methods. We're just proposing to start production with a different virus. It could be a relatively simple fix."

The research was supported in part by the Duke School of Medicine Whitehead Scholarship and the National Institutes of Health (T32-GM007184-41 and T32-CA009111).

19

Vaccines Help Animals Stay Healthy, Too

Health Europa

Health Europa is a website dedicated to reporting news about European health policy.

Humans are not the only living things that benefit from vaccinations. Animals, both pets and livestock, remain healthy when properly vaccinated. In many ways, vaccines given to animals are similar to the ones given to people and have the same preventative possibilities. So, vaccines are also good for pets and farm animals, the authors of the following viewpoint argue.

Treatment using vaccines is understood to be one of the greatest breakthroughs in modern medicine; no single medical intervention method has contributed more to the reduction of fatality and the improvement of quality of life. As a result of vaccinations, smallpox has been eradicated, whilst cases of polio are near eradication.

In a report from the World Health Organization, it states on the efficacy of vaccines: "Unless an environmental reservoir exists, an eradicated pathogen cannot re-emerge, unless accidentally or malevolently reintroduced by humans, allowing vaccination or other preventative methods to be discontinued."

Although the efficacy of vaccination is high, diminished recognition of their vast importance poses a threat, whereby

"Vaccines for Animal and Human Health," Pan European Networks Ltd, August 3, 2018. Reprinted by permission.

reduced vaccination rates could see the return of fatal diseases and viruses. In this article, Health Europa explores how vaccines have benefitted not only humans but also animals, whilst limiting the transmission of zoonotic diseases.

How Are Animal Vaccines Preventing the Transmission of Zoonotic Diseases?

The vaccination of pets and farm animals is essential in order to maintain good animal health and welfare, whilst also reducing the disease burden in pets and livestock. As mutations of infection and disease develop, the role of vaccines in preventative treatment and disease control programmes is integral. With a long and successful history of preventing and controlling disease, the veterinary vaccines of today are symbolic of years of cutting-edge research but also represent the diseases faced by pets and livestock.

In order to prevent disease, animals are vaccinated to reduce suffering and the transmission of micro-organisms amongst the animal populous. Vaccination is also predominantly a more cost-efficient treatment pathway than treating sick animals. Whilst pets receive vaccines for infections such as rabies, parvovirus distemper and hepatitis, livestock—turkeys, chicken, cattle and pigs—is vaccinated against diseases such as rotavirus, E. coli, pinkeye and brucellosis. By vaccinating pets and livestock, people and herds can be kept healthy.

Another means of protecting livestock is that of herd immunity, whereby protection is provided to larger communities of animals (who may not all be vaccinated) in which a large majority are vaccinated, thus reducing the prevalence of a given disease and those susceptible within an area.

How Do Vaccines Take Effect?

Vaccinations take effect through stimulation of the animal's immune system without causing the disease, enabling that animal to be prevented from catching the disease. Once an animal is vaccinated, its immune system responds and can, subsequently, remember the infectious agent which the animal is protected against and provide a sufficient level of protection against the disease, should the animal come into contact with that same agent.

Regardless of the vaccination provided, animals should be in a state of good health, as a properly functioning immune system is required in order to stimulate an effective immune response and to develop the necessary level of protection.

In the initial stages of the treatment process, a primary vaccination course is completed, but, depending on the vaccine type and species targeted, it may be necessary to have additional booster vaccinations at intervals in order to maintain protective immunity throughout an animal's lifetime. As animals are exposed to a range of varying risks, related to age, lifestyle, disease threats and migration/travel, vaccination protocols are tailored by veterinarians for an individual animal or a group of animals.

What Types of Vaccine Are There?

Today's vaccines are categorised into:

- Modified-live (attenuated);
- Inactivated;
- Recombinant; and
- Toxoid.

Modified-Live (Attenuated) Vaccines

Modified-live vaccinations are characterised by an intact, but weakened, pathogen contained inside the vaccine, which stimulates an immune response but does not cause clinical disease.

Inactivated (Killed) Vaccines

An inactivated vaccine contains an inactivated pathogen, meaning that it is no longer infectious. Such vaccines frequently contain an adjuvant—a compound added in order to strengthen the protective immune response.

Recombinant Vaccines

Recombinant vaccines are produced through genetic engineering technology. They utilise genetic material from the desired pathogen in order to produce proteins which stimulate an immune response upon vaccination.

Toxoid Vaccines

Toxoid vaccines encompass inactivated toxins that are produced by pathogens. As a result, these vaccines protect an animal against toxins through stimulation of immunity, which, in turn, protects the animal.

Stopping the Transmission of Zoonotic Disease

But it is not only animals who are at risk when vaccinations are not made; public health amongst humans is also protected through vaccination of animals. Before entering, or returning, to the UK, animals such as cats, dogs and ferrets are required to show that they have a valid rabies vaccination. As one of the most prevalent and fatal zoonoses, vaccination is integral in protecting both animals and people in the UK from the threat of rabies.

Since the first course of rabies treatment was administered in the 19th century by Louis Pasteur, rabies vaccines have been benefitted by developments in both production and control. Since then, vaccines for human use have seen a transition from vaccines being prepared from animal nerve tissue to embryonated eggs to cultures of human diploid cells (HDC) around 1960. This vaccine remains the reference in comparative studies of immunogenicity.

Refining the Rabies Vaccine for Humans

In 1964, an inactivated rabies vaccine for human administration was prepared in cell culture, and in 1966 it was shown that the HDC strain W1-38 was an appropriate substrate for the propagation of the Pitman-Moore strain of fixed rabies virus. Since 1967, R&D on the vaccine has been led at the Mérieux Institute, Lyon, France.

Despite its safety and high immunogenicity, the low titre of virus production from these cells led to limitations on large-scale production, where a more cost-effective rabies vaccines of the same quality was available. The inactivated poliomyelitis vaccine was the first using this cell substrate and subsequently led to the revision of requirements for such a vaccine by the World Health Organization Expert Committee on Biological Standardization.

The technique was developed by Van Wezel and consisted of exploring the culture of cells on microcarriers, stimulating large-scale cultures of cells for human vaccine preparation. Following the production of an inactivated poliomyelitis vaccine in Vero cells, studies were conducted in an effort to develop a human rabies vaccine. As a result, the purified Vero cell rabies vaccine (PVRV) was produced, but it required a purification step in order to remove residual cellular DNA.

A purified chick-embryo cell vaccine for administration in humans is prepared using chick embryo cells and derived from specific pathogen-free (SPF) eggs. The vaccine is developed using freeze-dried preparation, which consists of purified and concentrated rabies virus antigen inactivated with B-propiolactone.

Reducing the Threat of Fatal Disease

Owing to the introduction of a childhood vaccination programme by the NHS in the UK, children of the UK are now protected against many dangerous diseases, including: smallpox, polio, diphtheria and whooping cough.

In 18th century Europe, smallpox was responsible for killing thousands; the disease was capable of killing around a third of victims, whilst leaving survivors scarred or blinded. However, in 1980, smallpox was successfully eradicated. Had a vaccine not been developed, smallpox could have caused an estimated two million death every year globally.

Meanwhile, polio has been eradicated from the majority of the world, including within the UK, Europe, the Western Pacific and the Americas. The disease is caused by a virus that destroys nerve cells and, at its peak, threatened millions of people worldwide. Furthermore, up to one in every 1,000 children and one in 75 adults who caught the infection were paralysed, affecting not only patients' arms and legs but breathing muscles, leading to a rise in the risk of suffocation. As a result, the only way to alleviate the complications caused by polio-induced respiratory conditions was to place them in an iron lung, assisting them with breathing.

In 1940, diphtheria was responsible for more than 60,000 cases and around 3,000 deaths within the UK alone. By 2002, vaccines had almost eradicated this disease entirely, to the extent whereby the death toll of diphtheria was reduced to two between 1986 and 2002.

Since the introduction of a vaccine in the UK in 1999, meningitis C has been virtually eliminated. The first country to offer vaccination against meningitis C, the UK has seen a 99% reduction in cases of meningitis C in patients under 20 since the vaccination was developed and provided.

Owing to the provision of vaccines, such diseases are now either extremely rare or eradicated. Although these diseases may be rare currently, if children aren't vaccinated, such diseases are able to return with the same threat to the population.

Progressing Vaccination Programmes

Cutting-edge research and development of safe, high-efficacy, high-quality vaccines means that pets and farm animals remain able to benefit from crucial medicines that may prevent or alleviate the clinical signs and stages of disease. R&I has led to the development of novel, highly sophisticated technologies, one example being marker vaccines. Traditional vaccination approaches that seek to protect animals evoke an immune response that is similar to that of a natural infection. Therefore, when testing, this causes complications in differentiating between those animals that have been infected and those that are vaccinated. The livestock marker vaccine for infectious bovine rhinotracheitis (IBR)—a highly contagious respiratory disease affecting cattle—is just one example of the cutting-edge outcomes made possible by RD&I.

Today, research continues to thrive, and more than 150 innovative vaccines are in the testing phase. It is anticipated that an improved pneumococcal vaccine will soon be available, offering an increased level of protection against more strains of pneumonia, whilst promising research continues on exploring vaccines for flu, which remains active for extended periods of time.

Organizations to Contact

The editors have compiled the following list of organizations concerned with the issues debated in this book. The descriptions are derived from materials provided by the organizations. All have publications or information available for interested readers. The list was compiled on the date of publication of the present volume; the information provided here may change. Be aware that many organizations take several weeks or longer to respond to inquiries, so allow as much time as possible.

American Red Cross—Measles & Rubella Initiative
431 18th Street NW
Washington, DC 20006
(800) 733-2767
email: Use form on contact page.
website: www.redcross.org/about-us/our-work/international
-services/measles-and-rubella-initiative.html

The American Red Cross is an organization dedicated to helping others in the US and around the world. The agency is playing a key part to fight preventable disease, and the Measles & Rubella Initiative website has information about disease and vaccination.

Centers for Disease Control and Prevention (CDC)
1600 Clifton Road
Atlanta, GA 30329
(800) 232-4636
email: Use link on contact page.
website: www.cdc.gov

The CDC is intent on protecting Americans from threats to their health. The agency conducts scientific work and provides the information to the public. Get trusted information from the site about vaccines and the diseases prevented by vaccination.

College of Physicians of Philadelphia
19 S 22nd Street
Philadelphia, PA 19103
(215) 563-3737
email: info@collegeofphysicians.org
website: www.collegeofphysicians.org

The College of Physicians of Philadelphia is a professional medical organization. It is committed to advancing the cause of health in the US. The agency believes in enabling individuals, families, and communities to be active in controlling their health, and so it maintains educational materials about the safety and appropriateness of vaccines.

Foundation for Economic Education (FEE)
1819 Peachtree Road NE, Suite 300
Atlanta, GA 30309
(404) 554-9980
email: Use form on contact page.
website: https://fee.org

FEE's mission is to inspire and connect future leaders with the principles of a free society. The organization has a large searchable database. Articles focus on vaccines and vaccinations from a libertarian point of view.

Healthline
40 West 25th Street, 5th Floor
New York, NY 10010
(917) 720-4400
email: Use link on contact page.
website: www.healthline.com

Healthline is an online newsletter covering a variety of health topics. It has current information about health topics, including vaccines and vaccinations. Information is delivered through articles, online interactive tools, short videos, and more.

National Institutes of Health (NIH)
9000 Rockville Pike
Bethesda, MD 20892
(301) 496-4000
website: www.nih.gov

The NIH is a governmental agency under the US Department of Health and Human Services. The difference is that this organization is responsible for medical research. It provides access to information about almost any health topic. Articles, links to other websites, newsletters, checklists, and more provide trusted information.

National Vaccine Information Center (NVIC)
21525 Ridgetop Circle, Suite 100
Sterling, VA 20166
(703) 938-0342
email: contactNVIC@gmail.com
website: www.nvic.org

The NVIC in a nonprofit clearinghouse with information about policy, law, and vaccine science. The agency is dedicated to preventing vaccine injuries and deaths. The staff maintains the website so individuals can find trusted information about vaccines.

US Department of Health and Human Services (HHS)
200 Independence Avenue SW
Washington, DC 20201
(877) 696-6775
email: See links on contact page.
website: www.hhs.gov

The HHS seeks to improve the health and well-being of all Americans. Find up-to-date information about vaccines and vaccinations. This website also provides links to other helpful organizations.

US Food and Drug Administration (FDA)
10903 New Hampshire Avenue
Silver Spring, MD 20993-0002
(888) 463-6332
email: Use links on contact page.
website: www.fda.gov/home

The FDA is a US governmental agency that is charged with protecting the health of the American public. This encompasses a wide array of work, including that of making sure that vaccines, biological products, and medical devices are safe for both humans and animals.

Vaccinate Your Family (VYF)
1012 14th Street NW, Suite 415
Washington, DC 20005
(202) 783-7034
email: info@vaccinateyourfamily.org
website: www.vaccinateyourfamily.org

VYF is a nonprofit organization that has a mission to protect people of all ages from vaccine-preventable diseases. Find a wide variety of educational materials about vaccines and vaccinations on this site, including articles, videos, and webinars.

World Health Organization (WHO)
Avenue Appia 20
1202 Geneva
Switzerland
email: See links on contact page.
website: www.who.int

WHO is a worldwide health organization of people from over 150 countries. Through information, including the vast array of resources on its website, this organization seeks to dispel the myth and misinformation surrounding vaccines and vaccinations.

Bibliography

Books

Sarah Bridges, *A Bad Reaction: A Memoir*. New York, NY: Skyhorse Publishing, 2016.

Elena Conis, *Vaccine Nation: America's Changing Relationship with Immunization*. Chicago, IL: University of Chicago Press, 2015.

Kristen A. Feemster, *Vaccines: What Everyone Needs to Know*. Oxford, UK: Oxford University Press, 2018.

Tara Haelle, *Vaccination Investigation: The History and Science of Vaccines*. Minneapolis, MN: Twenty-First Century Books, 2018.

Peter J. Hotez, *Vaccines Did Not Cause Rachel's Autism: My Journey as a Vaccine Scientist, Pediatrician, and Autism Dad*. Baltimore, MD: Johns Hopkins University Press, 2018.

Michael S. Kinch, *Between Hope and Fear: A History of Vaccines and Human Immunity*. New York, NY: Pegasus Books, 2018.

Louise Murray, *Vet Confidential: An Insider's Guide to Protecting Your Pet's Health*. New York, NY: Ballantine Books, 2008.

Paul A. Offit, *Deadly Choices: How the Anti-Vaccine Movement Threatens Us All*. New York, NY: Basic Books, 2011.

Jennifer A. Reich, *Calling the Shots: Why Parents Reject Vaccines*. New York, NY: New York University Press, 2016.

John Rhodes, *The End of Plagues: The Global Battle Against Infectious Disease*. New York, NY: Palgrave Macmillan, 2013.

Rebecca Rissman, *The Vaccination Debate*. Edina, MN: Essential Library, 2016.

Meredith Wadman, *The Vaccine Race: Science, Politics, and the Human Costs of Defeating Disease*. New York, NY: Viking, 2017.

Periodicals and Internet Sources

Jason Beaubien, "U.S. Measles Outbreaks Are Driven by a Global Surge in the Virus," NPR, April 30, 2019. https://www.npr.org/sections/goatsandsoda/2019/04/30/717473521/u-s-measles-outbreak-is-linked-to-global-surge-in-the-virus.

Helen Branswell, "It's Old News That Vaccines Don't Cause Autism," STAT, March 4, 2019. https://www.statnews.com/2019/03/04/vaccines-no-association-autism-major-study.

Patrick A. Coleman, "Reminder: Jenny McCarthy Helped Cause the Anti-Vaxxer Measles Outbreak," Fatherly, February 7, 2019. https://www.fatherly.com/health-science/jenny-mccarthy-masked-singer-measles-outbreak-anti-vaxxer.

Donald G. McNeil Jr., "Measles Cases Surpass 700 as Outbreak Continues Unabated," *New York Times*, April 29, 2019. https://www.nytimes.com/2019/04/29/health/measles-outbreak-cdc.html.

Tim Newman, "MMR Vaccine Does Not Cause Autism, Even in Those at Most Risk," *Medical News Today*, March 7, 2019. https://www.medicalnewstoday.com/articles/324619.php.

Karin Roberts, "When It Comes to Vaccines, Celebrities Often Call the Shots," NBC News, October 28, 2018. https://www.nbcnews.com/health/health-care/when-it-comes-vaccines-celebrities-often-call-shots-n925156.

Hub Staff, "The Science Is Clear: Vaccines Are Safe, Effective, and Do Not Cause Autism," Johns Hopkins University, January 11, 2017. https://hub.jhu.edu/2017/01/11/vaccines-autism-public-health-expert.

Index